Pocket Rough Guide

Reykjavík

written and researched by

DAVID LEFFMAN AND JAMES PROCTOR

D1026201

Contents

INTRODUCTION TO

Reykjavík

If you're more used to the traffic-clogged streets of other major European cities, Reykjavík's sense of space and calm will come as a breath of fresh air. That said, the world's most northerly capital still dwarfs Iceland's other built-up areas, with the Greater Reykjavík area home to two out of every three Icelanders. The atmosphere generated by this bustling port, with its highbrow museums, colourful streets and buzzing nightlife, has earned the city a reputation for hedonistic revelry which draws visitors from across the globe, in record-breaking numbers – and its popularity shows no signs of waning.

AUSTURVÖLLUR

Best places to swim

Reykjavík has several excellent swimming pools to choose from. The biggest is Laugardalslaug, with outdoor pools and hot pots (see p.75). When extension work is complete, Sundhöllin (see p.129) will boast a large new outdoor pool, in addition to its exisiting indoor one. It also has hot pots and sun terraces. Most visitors can't wait to try the geothermal hot pots and sea lagoon at Nauthólsvík, where there's also a glorious sandy beach (see p.72). Wherever you swim, you must shower thoroughly without a swimming costume before entering the water, since it is not treated with chlorine.

Split roughly into two halves by the brilliant waters of Tjörnin lake, the tiny city centre is more a place to amble around and take in the suburban-looking streets and corner cafés than somewhere to hurtle about, ticking off attractions. Reykjavík lacks the grand and imposing buildings found in other Nordic capitals, possessing instead apparently ramshackle clusters of houses, either clad in garishly painted corrugated iron or daubed in pebbledash as protection against the ferocious North Atlantic storms. This rather unkempt feel, though, is as much part of the city's charm as the views across the sea to glaciers and the sheer mountains that form the backdrop to the streets. Even in the heart of this capital, nature is always in evidence –

there can be few other cities in the world, for example, where greylag geese regularly overfly the busy centre, sending bemused visitors, more accustomed to pigeons, scurrying for cover.

Amid the essentially residential city centre, it is the Hallgrímskirkja, a gargantuan white concrete church towering over the surrounding houses, that is the most enduring image of Reykjavík. Below this, the elegant shops and stylish bars and restaurants that line the main street and commercial thoroughfare of Laugavegur are a consumer's heaven. The central core of streets around Laugavegur and Skólavörðustígur is where you'll find a range of engaging museums, too. The displays in the Landnámssýning and the Saga Museum, for example,

When to visit

celandic weather is notoriously unpredictable. In summer, Reykjavík tends to be cloudy and showery, though there can be long, clear spells of sunny weather, too. However, one thing is consistent – it's never really warm. Summer in Reykjavík is more about the long daylight hours than a sudden surge in temperature – the average summer range in the city is 8–14°C. Since Reykjavík lies south of the Arctic Circle, it doesn't experience true Midnight Sun, though nights are light from mid-May to early August. Conversely, in winter, days are short and dark – at the shortest time of the year, in December, the sun doesn't rise until around 10.30–11am, setting again just a couple of hours later. Between September and January, there's a good chance of seeing the Northern Lights. During winter, storms are frequent and temperatures tend to hover a few degrees either side of freezing point.

offer an accessible introduction to Iceland's stirring past; while whale-watching and puffin-spotting tours from the city harbour give you a chance to experience Icelandic nature up close.

With time to spare, it's worth venturing outside the city limits to explore some of southwest Iceland's greatest attractions. Top of everyone's list is the erupting geyser known as Strokkur, and the nearby rift valley, Þingvellir, where you can see a clear split in the earth's tectonic plates; both are easily accessible on day-trips from the capital. A little further afield, the Westman Islands, scene of the famous 1973 eruption, beckon enticingly, while the rugged natural beauty of Þorsmörk national park and the Landmannalaugar geothermal springs, which mark the jumping-off point into Iceland's remote and uninhabited Interior, are equally worthy of your time.

REYKJAVÍK AT A GLANCE

>> EATING

The one thing every visitor remembers about a visit to Reykjavík is eating the freshest fish they have ever tasted. In fact, there are many Icelanders who simply refuse to order fish when they travel abroad, because it doesn't taste like it does at home. In recent years there's been a veritable explosion in the number of fish restaurants in Reykjavík, serving unusual offerings such as catfish and blue ling alongside more common species like cod and haddock. The other Icelandic staple is mountain lamb, which is as succulent as you would expect, and available in most restaurants. Look out for lunchtime specials (often set menus) when prices are much lower than you will pay in the evening.

>> DRINKING

Drinking in Reykjavík is expensive. However, there are several ways to cut costs. Consider buying wine, beer or spirits on arrival, at the duty-free store inside Keflavík airport. Ask the helpful staff about your duty-free allowances. Alternatively, buy your booze from the state-run alcohol stores, *vínbúðin*, dotted across the city, where prices are higher than at duty free but less than in bars and restaurants. Of course, having a drink in a bar is also tempting – to cut costs, look out for happy hours when prices on alcohol are slashed. Drinking with food in a café or restaurant, though, can soon add up.

>> NIGHTLIFE

Reykjavík is deservedly known for its nightlife. Although the scene is actually no bigger than that of any small-sized town in most other countries, what sets it apart is the northerly setting and location for all this revelry – during the light nights of summer, it's very disorientating to have entered a nightclub in the wee small hours with the sun just about to set, only to emerge a couple of hours later into the blinding and unflattering daylight of the Icelandic morning. The bars and clubs of Austurstræti, Hafnarstræti and Laugavegur are likely to be where you'll spend your time. It can be fun to join in when clubbers spill out into Lækjartorg early on Saturday and Sunday mornings for an alfresco end to the night.

>> SHOPPING

Reykjavík's main thoroughfare, Laugavegur, and the Kringlan shopping centre are where you'll find most of the city's shops. That said, Skólavörðustígur is beginning to ramp up its act and now comes a close second to Laugavegur. Remember that most goods are available at tax-free prices when exported from Iceland – ask in store when browsing for details of the cash refund you're entitled to (see p.133). Particularly good-value purchases include anything made of wool – from traditional sweaters, gloves and scarves to blankets, shawls and hats.

OUR RECOMMENDATIONS FOR WHERE TO EAT, DRINK AND SHOP ARE LISTED AT THE END OF EACH CHAPTER.

Day One in Reykjavík

1 **Whales of Iceland** > p.46. Begin the day checking out the life-size, silicone models of the whales found in Icelandic waters and learn all about these giants of the sea.

2 **Whale watching** > p.47. Head down to the harbour and go in search of the real thing on a whale-watching tour off the Reykjavík coast.

🍴 **Lunch** > p.34. An easy walk from the harbour, *Apótek* serves a good-value fishy lunch, amid a beautifully appointed interior.

3 **Þjóðminjasafnið** > p.52. Get to grips with Iceland's stirring past at the National Museum, whose exhibitions on medieval church art and DNA testing are first class.

4 **Tjörnin** > p.50. From the National Museum, take a pleasant stroll back into the city centre along the banks of Tjörnin lake, for some great views of Reykjavík and its birdlife.

5 **Hallgrímskirkja** > p.64. Ride the lift to the top of the Hallgrímskirkja's tower for superlative views of the city and coastline, then check out the huge church organ.

6 **Sundhöllin** > p.129. From the church, walk down to Sundhöllin swimming pool, where you can swim, bathe in the hot pots, or even sunbathe on the sun terraces if the weather allows.

🍴 **Dinner** > p.61. Undoubtedly one of Reykjavík's most creative restaurants, *Friðrik V* features a fusion of Mediterranean and Icelandic flavours.

Day Two in Reykjavík

1 Landnámssýning > p.36.
Inspect the remains of a Viking-age
hall, still in its original location,
and learn all about the days of the
Settlement in this informative and
engaging museum.

2 Saga Museum > p.44. Put faces
to some of the names who featured
prominently during the Settlement
of Iceland – the wax models in this
museum are startlingly lifelike.

Lunch > p.42. Sample some
of the freshest fish you'll
ever taste at *Icelandic Fish & Chips*,
inside the Volcano House.

3 Volcano House > p.40. Watch
the films of Icelandic eruptions in
the Volcano House and witness the
disruptive power Icelanders live with on
a daily basis.

4 Laugavegur > p.59. Time for
some retail therapy: go for a wander
along the length of Laugavegur and
you might just succumb to the range of
goods on offer.

5 Hið Íslenzka Reðasafn > p.65.
At the eastern end of Laugavegur,
you'll find Reykjavík's most offbeat
museum – dedicated to the humble
penis. Examples of animal and human
members abound.

Dinner > p.48. Classic
Icelandic dishes are given
a modern makeover at *Matur og
Drykkur*, next to the Saga Museum.

6 Seafront stroll > p.66. Take a
post-dinner stroll along Sæbraut for
some great views of Mount Esja, as
well as a chance to see the *Sólfar*
statue and Höfði house.

Away from the crowds

Reykjavík is one of Europe's smaller and saner capitals. Escaping the crowds and finding a spot of peace and tranquillity is relatively easy.

1 Hafnarfjörður > p.80. Hop on the bus for the short ride to Hafnarfjörður, Reykjavík's southern neighbour. In comparison with the capital, the streets here are all but empty of visitors.

2 Viðey > p.78. For just 1100kr you can ride the ferry to Viðey for great views of Reykjavík and the surrounding coastline. Viðey boasts some great hiking trails, too, offering a real chance to commune with nature in the city.

3 Reykjanes Peninsula > p.84. With your own transport a drive around the southwestern point of the

Reykjanes Peninsula, through the lava landscapes between Gríndavík and Hafnir, is especially rewarding.

4 Öskjuhlíð > p.70. The forested slopes of this city park south of the centre are the perfect place to escape the crowds. Pack a picnic and find your own shady glade among the trees.

5 South of Hallgrímskirkja > p.64. The streets south of Hallgrímskirkja, notably Njarðargata, Baldursgata and Óðinsgata, are relatively unexplored by visitors to the city. A stroll here is a chance to see residential Reykjavík.

6 Sun terraces, Sundhöllin > p.129. Sheltered from the wind, the outdoor terraces at the swimming pool here are a wonderful spot to catch the rays (in the buff) on a warm day – and they're little known to visitors.

Eat and drink like a local

With a wide range of eating and drinking options, it can be hard to make a sound choice. Here, then, is how the locals do it.

1 Vínbúðin > p.34. Given the high prices for alcohol in Reykjavík's bar and restaurants, many Reykjavíkers simply drink at home instead. Buy your booze from the *vínbúðin* on Austurstræti and save a small fortune.

2 Mokka > p.69. This simple, understated café on Skólavörðustígur is a Reykjavík classic. It's been plying the people of the city with caffeine for years – and they can't get enough of it.

5 Vegamót > p.63. The weekend brunch specials at this long-standing locals' favourite really pull the crowds. *Vegamót* is not only good value but it's also a fun place to hang out.

6 Sandholt > p.61. Reykjavíkers claim this is the best café in the city. There's a great choice of takeaway pastries and sandwiches and its home-made chocolates are legend.

3 Ostabúðin > p.68. Drop in to this popular little delicatessen and buy some freshly baked bread and a few nibbles for a picnic lunch – you'll feel like you've lived in Reykjavík for years.

4 Happy hours > p.49, p.55 & p.69. Save money by drinking during the happy hours which are posted up outside many bars. A large beer can go for as little as 600kr – much less than you'd pay at home.

BEST OF REYKJAVIK

Museums

1 Þjóðminjasafnið The examples of medieval church art inside the National Museum are some of Iceland's finest treasures. **> p.52**

2 Landnámssýning Discover how Reykjavík's first settlers lived and see the extensive remains of a tenth-century Viking hall. > **p.36**

3 Saga Museum At Reykjavík's answer to Madame Tussauds, come face to face with the main characters of the Sagas – and even sample the smells of the Viking period. > **p.44**

4 Hafnarhúsið The cartoon-like work of Icelandic pop artist, Erró, is bold, vibrant and bursting with colour. > **p.40**

5 Ásmundarsafn Blending Mediterranean and North African motifs with elements from Icelandic legend, Ásmundur Sveinsson is one of Iceland's best-loved sculptors. > **p.76**

Viewpoints

1 **Hallgrímskirkja tower** The classic view of Reykjavík, with the city's multicoloured buildings laid out below you. > **p.64**

2 Harpa Unsurpassed views of the harbour area unfold from the top floor of the city's opera house. > **p.46**

4 Suðurgata Picture-postcard perfect, the views of Tjörnin and the vibrant colours of the houses of residential Reykjavík are a hit with photographers. > **p.51**

5 Perlan Panoramic views of the city and surrounding coastline, and the perfect place to see planes buzzing over the Reykjavík rooftops before landing at the City Airport. > **p.70**

3 Sæbraut With Mount Esja forming a magnificent backdrop, the views across the sea from Sæbraut help put Reykjavík in a geographical perspective. > **p.66**

Budget

1 **Nauthólsvík** Bathe in the sublime waters of Nauthólsvík geothermal lagoon and hot pots for free. **>** **p.72**

2 City bus ride See the sights of central Reykjavík from on board bus #12 for the price of a single ticket, or buy a multi-ride pass. > **p.127**

3 Ljósmindasafn Reykjavíkur Check out the engaging exhibitions in the city's museum of photography – there's no entry charge. > **p.39**

4 Out to lunch Eat as much as you want at the good-value fish buffet at *Sjávarbarinn* – it's just 1790kr, including soup and coffee, every lunchtime. > **p.49**

5 Öskjuhlíð Explore the footpaths which crisscross this wooded hill to the south of the city centre, and enjoy the views from its summit – either inside Perlan or outside. > **p.70**

Activities

1 **Whale watching** Regular boat tours depart from the city harbour to spot whales throughout the year. > **p.47**

2 Glacier tours They don't come cheap, but a trip to, onto and even into an Icelandic glacier is unforgettable. **> p.129**

3 Horseriding With their fifth gait – a cross between a trot and a canter, called *tölt* – riding an Icelandic horse is a unique experience. **> p.129**

4 Rúntur On Friday and Saturday nights, an extended pub crawl, the *rúntur*, draws crowds of drinkers – especially on March 1. **> p.134**

5 Shopping Selling at tax-free prices for export, many Reykjavík stores have some extremely competitive prices on international brands. **> p.133**

Waterfalls

1 Háifoss A half-day return hike is needed to reach this remote, attractive waterfall right on the border of the Interior. > **p.109**

2 Gullfoss One of the most popular tourist attractions in Iceland, the Hvítá cascades down a three-step staircase, before plunging, in two more stages, into a deep crevice. > **p.94**

3 Þjófafoss The vivid Þjórsá river feeds Þjófafoss falls, south of Búrfell mountain. > **p.110**

4 Seljalandsfoss Paths run behind the curtain of water at these falls, giving a breathtaking perspective. > **p.99**

5 Skógarfoss A drop of over 60m makes this waterfall one of the most impressive in southern Iceland – particularly when viewed from the river bed. > **p.102**

Great outdoors

1 Strokkur The erupting geyser that everyone wants to see – Strokkur shoots a spout of boiling water 30m into the air every few minutes. > **p.94**

2 Þingvellir See the rift valley where the Eurasian and North American tectonic plates are literally tearing apart. > **p.90**

3 Þórsmörk A beautifully wooded highland valley surrounded by glaciers, perfect for camping and hiking. > **p.112**

4 Volcanic beach, Vík Forget any notion of golden strands – along the south coast, beaches are composed of fine black volcanic sand. > **p.103**

5 Hekla Iceland's second most active volcano – and the one everyone can actually spell. Its earliest recorded eruption was in 1104, and it's still at it. > **p.110**

Thermal pools

1 Landmannalaugar The quintessential Icelandic experience – bathing in a geothermal hot spring amid wilderness landscapes which ooze rugged grandeur.
> p.110

2 Blue Lagoon Lolling around in the geothermal, silica-rich waters here is not just relaxing – it's also extremely good for your skin. > **p.84**

3 Hveragerði Take a hike out from the little town of Hveragerði, which sits atop an active geothermal area, to this warm shallow stream. > **p.96**

4 Fontana spa, Laugarvatn Built over a natural hot spring, this spa features three steam rooms, a sauna, hot pot, swimming pool and a longer, shallow bathing pool. > **p.92**

5 Laugardalslaug Iceland's biggest and best swimming pool. There's a 50m outdoor pool, plus smaller children's pools, as well as several hot pots. > **p.75**

PLACES

Lækjartorg, Austurstræti and Austurvöllur

The best place to get your first taste of Reykjavík is around Lækjartorg and the adjoining pedestrianized Austurstræti on the square's western side. This area is a general meeting place for Reykjavík's urbanites, where people stroll, strut and sit on benches munching cakes, ice creams and burgers bought from the nearby fast-food outlets and the 10–11 supermarket. If Reykjavík has a main square, meanwhile, it is Austurvöllur, a more stately – though still diminutive – space south of Austurstræti that is home to the Icelandic parliament, Reykjavík cathedral and a handful of imposing buildings, including the city's very first hotel, *Hótel Borg*, dating from the 1930s.

LÆKJARTORG

MAP PP.32–33, POCKET MAP D4

This square has always been at the heart of Reykjavík life; indeed, it was here that farmers bringing produce to market ended their long journey from the surrounding countryside and set up camp to sell their goods. Although the Icelandic name does indeed mean "square" ("brook square", in fact, named after the stream which flows beneath it), Lækjartorg is not the kind of grand, imposing place you might find elsewhere in Europe: it is more a wide, paved pedestrian entrance to Austurstræti. Despite its modest appearance, however, this can be one of the most boisterous areas in the city. On Friday and Saturday evenings, particularly in summer, hundreds of drunken revellers fill the square when the clubs empty out at 4 or 5am, jostling for prime position – the noise from the good-hearted throng can be deafening.

AUSTURSTRÆTI

MAP PP.32–33, POCKET MAP C3

By day, Austurstræti has a busy commercial air as people dash in and out of the post office, pop in to the Eymundsson bookshop and sort out money matters at the main branch of Landsbanki. Beyond its junction with Pósthússtræti, the road gives itself over solely to pleasure, as this is where some of the city's best bars and restaurants can be found. Austurstræti is also the location for the *vínbúð* **state alcohol store**, a futuristic glass-and-steel structure at number 10a, where those who want to drink at home have to come to buy their alcohol supplies.

AUSTURVÖLLUR

MAP PP.32–33, POCKET MAP C4

Pósthússtræti, running south from Austurstræti, leads into another small square, Austurvöllur, a favourite place for city slickers from nearby

Icelandic people power

Every Saturday between October 2008 and January 2009, thousands of Icelanders gathered in Austurvöllur to voice their anger over the collapse of the Icelandic banking system which, it's estimated, left one in five families bankrupt. The protesters burned the flag of Landsbanki (one of the country's leading banks) and were soon also calling for heads to roll. The main target of popular discontent was the leader of the Icelandic Central Bank and former long-serving politician, Davið Oddsson, who was squarely blamed for the economic collapse, and was replaced as the head of the bank in March 2009. The demonstrators became more vocal as the lack of decisive action by the government continued, with three and a half months of protests in Austurvöllur and at various locations around the country, finally convincing Prime Minister Geir Haarde that his administration had no future; to national jubilation, it fell on January 26, 2009. Today, thanks to the square's central position and the fact that any number of MPs regularly trot through on their way to parliamentary sessions, this remains Iceland's favourite place for demonstrators to harangue the government.

offices to catch a few rays during their lunch breaks, stretched out on the grassy lawns edged with flowers. The square's modest proportions and nondescript apartment blocks, meanwhile, somewhat belie its historical importance: this was the site of the farm of Reykjavík's first settler, **Ingólfur Arnarson**; it's thought he grew his hay on the land where the square now stands, and it marks the original centre of the city. Similarly, the square's central, elevated statue of the nineteenth-century independence campaigner **Jón Sigurðsson**, entitled *The Pride of Iceland, its Sword and Shield*, faces two of the most important buildings in the country – the Alþingi and the Dómkirkjan – though you'd never realize their status from their appearance.

AUSTURVÖLLUR

Lækjartorg, Austurstræti and Austurvöllur

SHOPS
Eymundsson	2
Nordic Store	3
Vínbúðin	1

CAFÉS & RESTAURANTS
Apótek	5
Café Paris	4
Einar Ben	2
Grillmarkaðurinn	6
Laundromat Café	3
Nora Magasin	7
Restaurant Reykjavík	1

BARS
Bjarni Fell	3
English Pub	2
Micro Bar	1

ACCOMMODATION
Borg	5
Plaza	1
Radisson Blu 1919	2
Reykjavík Centrum	3
Salvation Army Guesthouse	4

ALÞINGISHÚSIÐ

Austurvöllur Square. Closed to the public.
MAP PP.32–33, POCKET MAP C4

The Alþingishúsið (Parliament Building) is ordinary in the extreme, a slight building made of grey basalt quarried from nearby Skólavörðuholt hill, with the date of its completion (1881) etched into its dark frontage – yet this unremarkable structure played a pivotal role in bringing about Icelandic independence. In 1798, the parliament moved to Reykjavík from Þingvellir (see p.90), where it had been operating virtually without interruption since 930 AD. Within just two years, however, it was dissolved as Danish power reached its peak. Yet after much struggle, the Alþingi regained its powers from Copenhagen as a consultative body in 1843, and a constitution was granted in

1874 which made Iceland self-governing in domestic affairs. The **Act of Union**, passed in this building in 1918, made Iceland a sovereign state under the Danish Crown, but by 1940 Denmark was occupied by the Nazis and the Alþingi had assumed the duties normally carried out by the monarch, declaring its intention to dissolve the Act of Union at the end of the war. Today, the modest interior, illuminated by chandeliers, more resembles a town council chamber than the seat of a national parliament.

DÓMKIRKJAN

Lækjargata 14a. Mon–Fri 10am–4.30pm. Free.
MAP PP.32–33, POCKET MAP D4

Reykjavík's Lutheran cathedral, the Dómkirkjan, is a Neoclassical stone structure partly shrouded in corrugated

iron to protect it from the weather. It was built between 1787 and 1796 after Christian VII of Denmark scrapped the Catholic bishoprics of Hólar in the north and Skálholt in the south, in favour of a Lutheran diocese in what was fast growing into Iceland's main centre of population. The church may be plain on the outside, but venture within and you'll discover a beautiful interior: perfectly designed arched windows punctuate the unadorned white-painted walls at regular intervals, giving an impression of complete architectural harmony. The cathedral is now deemed too small for great gatherings and services of state, and the roomier Hallgrímskirkja (see p.64) is preferred for state funerals and other such well-attended functions, although the **opening of**

parliament is still marked with a service in the Dómkirkjan followed by a short procession along Kirkjustræti to the Alþingishúsið.

DÓMKIRKJAN

Shops

EYMUNDSSON

Austurstræti 18 ☎ 540 2130, ⓦ eymundsson
.is. Mon-Sat 9am–10pm, Sun 10am–10pm.
MAP PP.32–33, POCKET MAP D4

The best bookshop in Reykjavík
with a good selection of books
about Iceland in English as well
as videos, postcards and other
souvenirs to take home.

NORDIC STORE

Lækjargata 2 ☎ 445 8080, ⓦ nordicstore.net.
Daily 9am–10pm. MAP PP.32–33, POCKET MAP D4

A one-stop shop for anything
woollen, including traditional
Icelandic sweaters. Eiderdown
duvets are also available and
home shipping offered.

VÍNBÚÐIN

Austurstræti 10a ☎ 562 6511, ⓦ vinbudin.is.
Mon-Thurs & Sat 11am–6pm, Fri 11am–7pm.
MAP P.32–33, POCKET MAP C4

A handily located branch of
the state alcohol monopoly.
Remember that booze is sold
exclusively at *vínbúðin* – you'll
search in vain elsewhere.

Cafés and
restaurants

APÓTEK

Austurstræti 16 ☎ 551 0011, ⓦ apotek.is.
Mon-Thurs 11.30am–11pm, Fri 11.30am–
midnight, Sat noon–midnight, Sun
noon–11.30pm. MAP PP.32–33, POCKET MAP D4

Once Reykjavík's main
apothecary, this stylish
restaurant specializes in fresh
seafood given a modern twist.
The set lunches (2790–3290kr)
represent a good deal.

CAFÉ PARIS

Austurstræti 14 ☎ 551 1020, ⓦ cafeparis.is.
Daily: May–Aug 8am–1am; Sept–April
9am–1am. MAP PP.32–33, POCKET MAP D4

Long gone are the days when
this was virtually the only café
in town. Since it opened in
1992, the French-style *Café
Paris* has become a Reykjavík
fixture, with outdoor seating
overlooking the Alþingi in
summer. Daily brunch for
2650kr, as well as excellent
crêpes and salads.

EINAR BEN

Veltusund 1 ☎ 511 5090, ⓦ einarben.is.
Tues–Fri 5.30–11pm, Sat & Sun 5–11pm.
MAP PP.32–33, POCKET MAP C3

Named after the poet Einar
Benediktsson, this handsome
place is heavy with chandeliers
and red drape curtains. The
menu is creative, offering the
likes of pan-fried salmon with
butternut purée (4200kr), or cod
fillet with tomato concassé, feta
cheese and ginger (also 4200kr).
An early-bird two-course special
is available until 7pm for 3950kr.

GRILLMARKAÐURINN

Lækjargata 2a ☎ 571 7777, ⓦ grillmarkadurinn.
is. Mon–Fri 11.30am–2pm & 6–10.30pm, Sat &
Sun 6–11.30pm. MAP PP.32–33, POCKET MAP D4

Everything served here – from
salmon and cod to steaks,
burgers and vegetables – is
sourced from local farmers and
fishermen and cooked on the
custom-made charcoal grill.
The stylish decor features lots
of stone and wood.

EINAR BEN

LAUNDROMAT CAFÉ

Austurstræti 9 ☎ 587 7555, ⓦ thelaundromat
cafe.com. Mon–Thurs 8am–midnight, Fri
8am–1am, Sat 9am–1am, Sun 9am–midnight.
MAP PP.32–33. POCKET MAP C3

The walls of this café are
covered with maps and the bar
is made of bookshelves lined
with paperbacks. On the menu
are burgers, salads, soups and
sandwiches, plus breakfast
options. Oh, and there's a
laundry on site, too.

NORA MAGASIN

Pósthússtræti 9 ☎ 578 2010, ⓦ facebook
.com/noramagasin. Mon–Thurs & Sun
11.30am–1am, Fri & Sat 11.30am–3am.
MAP PP.32–33, POCKET MAP D4

This place may be searching for
an identity when it comes to
decor – part family sitting
room and part trendy urban
bar – but the food is just plain
good: burgers (2290kr),
sandwiches (1650kr) and a
tasty fish of the day (2290kr).

RESTAURANT REYKJAVÍK

Vesturgata 2 ☎ 552 3030, ⓦ restaurant
reykjavik.is. Daily 5.30pm–late. MAP PP.32–33,
POCKET MAP C3

Although this restaurant
serves a wide and
accomplished menu, it's best
visited for its justifiably
renowned nightly fish buffet
(6750kr), which features all
manner of smoked, marinated,
baked and gratinated piscine
treats, plus a wide selection of
Icelandic cheeses.

Bars

BJARNI FEL

Austurstræti 20 ☎ 561 2240, ⓦ bjarnifel.is.
Mon–Thurs & Sun noon–1am, Fri & Sat
noon–4.30am. MAP PP.32–33, POCKET MAP D4

With its no-music policy, this
small and intimate sports bar,
full of memorabilia and TV

NORA MAGASIN

screens angled in all directions,
is the best place to catch the
latest football match over a cold
beer or two.

ENGLISH PUB

Austurstræti 12 ☎ 578 0400, ⓦ enskibar
inn.is. Mon–Thurs & Sun noon–1am, Fri & Sat
noon–5am. MAP PP.32–33, POCKET MAP D4

This is an attempt to create a
British-style pub in the heart
of Reykjavík – while the
interior is none too genuine,
there's lager, Guinness and
Kilkenny on draught, lots of
footie on TV and weekend live
music. You can also spin the
"wheel of fortune", with up to
eight free beers as the prize if
you win.

MICRO BAR

Austurstræti 6 ☎ 847 9084, ⓦ citycenter
hotel.is. Daily 4pm–12.30am. MAP PP.32–33,
POCKET MAP C3

Attached to the *City Center*
hotel, this place is a real treat.
It serves eighty or so different
beers from around the world,
plus a good selection produced
by some of Iceland's microbreweries. From pale ales to
barley wines, and stouts to
lagers, you're bound to find a
tipple to please.

Aðalstræti, Hafnarstræti and Tryggvagata

The trio of streets, Aðalstræti, Hafnarstræti and Tryggvagata, contains many of Reykjavík's bars and tourist-oriented shops. Don't confuse them, though, with the grand boulevards you might find in other capital cities; instead, they're modest affairs, barely a couple of hundred metres in length. Although they can't compete with Laugavegur, the city's main shopping street (see p.59), which is an altogether busier thoroughfare, these three are arguably a more pleasant place to stroll and linger. You'll doubtless end up spending time here either heading for the tourist office in Aðalstræti, sampling the shopping and bar culture or passing through on your way to the harbour. It's also where you'll find a couple of the city's museums, which come as a welcome addition to the shops and restaurants.

AÐALSTRÆTI

From the southwestern corner of Austurvöllur, Kirkjustræti runs the short distance to Reykjavík's oldest street, Aðalstræti, which follows the route taken in the late ninth century by Ingólfur Arnarson (see p.31) from his farm at the southern end of the street down to the sea. In addition to the remains of a Viking-age farmhouse on display inside the Landnámssýning museum, Aðalstræti also holds Reykjavík's **oldest surviving building**, a squat timber structure at no. 10. It dates back to 1752, and has served as a weaving shed, a bishop's residence and the home of Skúli Magnússon, High Sheriff of Iceland, who encouraged the development of craft industries here. On the opposite side of the street, a few steps north towards the sea outside the present no. 9, is Ingólfur Arnarson's freshwater well, **Ingólfsbrunnur**, which was discovered by fluke during road repairs here in 1992 and is now glassed over for posterity.

LANDNÁMSSÝNING AND THE SAGA EXHIBITION

Aðalstræti 16 ☎ 411 6372, ⓦ reykjavik871.is. Daily 9am–8pm. Settlement Exhibition 1400kr; Saga Exhibition 1000kr; 2200kr both exhibitions. MAP PP.38–39. POCKET MAP C4

The Landnámssýning (Settlement Exhibition), whose centrepiece is the extensive ruins of a **Viking-age farmhouse**, is one of Reykjavík's most remarkable museums. Housed in a purpose-built hall directly beneath Aðalstræti, the structure's oval-shaped stone walls, excavated in 2001, enclose a sizeable living space of 85 square metres, with a central hearth as the focal point. Dating the farmhouse has been quite straightforward,

AÐALSTRÆTI 10

since the layer of volcanic ash which fell across Iceland following a powerful eruption in around 871 AD lies just beneath the building; it's estimated, therefore, that people lived here between 930 and 1000. The exhibition's wall space is given over to panoramic views of forest and scrubland to convey a realistic impression of what Reykjavík would have looked like at the time of the Settlement. Indeed, when the first settlers arrived in the area, the hills were covered in birch woods. However, just one hundred years later, the birch had all but disappeared, felled to make way for grazing land or burnt for charcoal needed for iron-smelting. Housed in a side room to the left of reception, the **Saga Exhibition** is the place to see some of Iceland's medieval documents. Sadly, there are only five manuscripts on display here (the *Book of Icelanders*, the *Saga of the People of Kjalarnes*, the *Book of Settlements*, *Jónsbók* and the Deed of Purchase for Reykjavík from 1615) and you're bound to leave with your appetite

barely whetted. However, once construction of Hús íslenskra fræða (House of Icelandic Studies), opposite the National Museum (see p.52), is completed several years hence, this modest display will close and a more comprehensive exhibition will open in its place in the new building, which will also house the Árni Magnússon Institute, the keeper of Iceland's medieval manuscripts.

LANDNÁMSSÝNING

Aðalstræti

BARS
Dolly	4
Dubliner	3
Frederiksen Ale House	2
Gaukurinn	1

SHOPS
Kolaportið	1
Puffin	3
The Viking	2

CAFÉS & RESTAURANTS
Bæjarins beztu pylsur	5
Fish Market	7
Grillhúsið	4
Hornið	6
Icelandic Fish & Chips	3
Krua Thai	2
Reykjavik Fish Restaurant	1

HAFNARSTRÆTI

Many of the buildings on the south side of Hafnarstræti were formerly owned by Danish merchants during the Trade Monopoly of 1602–1855. Indeed, this street, as its name suggests (*hafnar* means "harbour"), once bordered the sea and gave access to the harbour, the city's economic lifeline and means of contact with the outside world. Today, Hafnarstræti is several blocks from the ocean, after landfill extended the city foreshore, and is home to some excellent bars and restaurants. Together with Austurstræti to the south and Tryggvagata to the north, it forms part of a rectangular block of cafés, restaurants and drinking holes that are well worth exploring.

FÁLKAHÚSIÐ

Corner of Aðalstræti and Hafnarstræti.
Opposite the tourist office, and covered in corrugated iron for protection, Fálkahúsið is another of Reykjavik's beautifully restored timber buildings, one of three in the city where the King of Denmark once kept his much-prized Icelandic falcons. Its turret-like side walls and sheer size still impress, especially when you consider the huge amount of timber that was imported for the job, as Iceland had no trees of its own. Cast an eye to the roof and you'll spot two carved wooden falcons still keeping guard over the building.

TRYGGVAGATA

Tryggvagata, one block north of the bustle of Hafnarstræti, is remarkable for a few things other than the number of

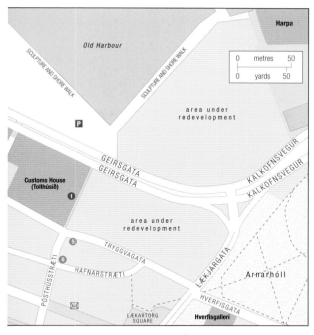

consonants in its name. The imposing, multicoloured mosaic **mural** by Gerður Helgadóttir (1928–75) close to its junction with Pósthússtræti portrays a busy harbour scene complete with fishing trawlers and cranes, and livens up the otherwise dull Tollhúsið (Customs House). Also along here are Ljósmindasafn Reykjavíkur – the Reykjavík Museum of Photography – and Hafnarhúsið, part of the Reykjavík Art Museum.

LJÓSMINDASAFN REYKJAVÍKUR

Tryggvagata 15 ☎ 411 6300,
🌐 ljosmyndasafnreykjavikur.is. Mon–Thurs noon–7pm, Fri noon–6pm, Sat & Sun 1–5pm. Free. MAP PP.38–39; POCKET MAP C2

The top floor of the city library building, **Grófarhús**, is given over to a changing exhibition of contemporary photography. Though the space is modest, the museum holds a collection of around six million photographs which it showcases alongside work from established visiting photographers. Moreover, the entire collection, which spans from 1870 to 2002, can now also be viewed online at 🌐 ljosmyndasafn.reykjavik.is /fotoweb/grid.fwx.

LJÓSMINDASAFN REYKJAVÍKUR

HAFNARHÚSIÐ

HAFNARHÚSIÐ

Tryggvagata 17 ☎ 590 1200, ⌨ artmuseum.is.
Daily 10am–5pm, Thurs till 8pm. 1400kr.
MAP PP.38–39, POCKET MAP C3

The large, austere Hafnarhúsið
(Harbour House) was
originally constructed in the
1930s as warehouse storage and
office space for the Port of
Reykjavík, but has now been
converted into six large
exhibition halls, connected by a
corridor running over a central
courtyard. The museum plays
host to frequently changing
displays of contemporary
Icelandic and international art,
with one permanent exhibition
dedicated to the multicoloured,
cartoon-like work of Icelandic
pop artist Erró. There's

certainly plenty of space here,
but the overall layout is a little
confusing, with an array of
corridors – which once linked
the former warehouse's storage
areas – that twist and turn
around the museum's
supporting concrete and
steel pillars.

VOLCANO HOUSE

Tryggvagata 11 ⌨ volcanohouse.is. Daily
10am–10pm. 1990kr. MAP PP.38–39, POCKET MAP C2

Unless you're of a serious
geological bent, it's unlikely
you'll to want to give but the
merest of glances to the lumps
of pumice, tephra and jasper
displayed here. Actually more
cinema than museum, the
Volcano House is worth
visiting mostly for the
twenty-minute films of the
1973 Westman Islands and
2010 Eyjafjallajökull eruptions,
shown every hour on the hour.
Although rather grainy, the
Westman Islands film is the
more interesting of the two,
documenting the devastating
impact of the eruption on the
island community. The
Eyjafjallajökull film, while
outlining the basics of what
happened geologically during
the eruption, barely mentions
the ensuing chaos in the skies
across Europe.

ART FOR SALE

With so much art on display in this relatively small city, it can be
tempting to purchase an original Icelandic work while you're in
Reykjavík. Should the urge strike, there are two galleries worth
checking out where you'll find a range of artists and styles represented: the
long-established i8, at Tryggvagata 18 (☎ 551 3666, ⌨ i8.is; Tues–Fri
11am–5pm, Sat 1–5pm; free) works with a group of around twenty artists, both
Icelandic and international, who produce contemporary fine art; at Hverfisgallerí,
just a couple of blocks away at Hverfisgata 4 (☎ 537 4007, ⌨ hverfisgalleri.is;
Tues–Fri 1–5pm, Sat & Sun 2–5pm; free), all bar one of the seventeen artists
represented are Icelandic, and the style is again contemporary fine art.
Exhibitions at both galleries tend to run for around five weeks.

THE VIKING

Shops

KOLAPORTIÐ

Tryggvagata 19 ☎ 562 5030, ⓦ kolaportid.is. Sat & Sun 11am–5pm. MAP PP.38–39, POCKET MAP D3

Iceland's biggest flea market is housed in a cavernous building between Tryggvagata and the sea where you'll find any number of secondhand and new items. There's also a food section where, among other things, you'll often find unusual delicacies such as shark meat.

PUFFIN

Hafnarstræti 5 ☎ 519 6070, ⓦ lundinn.is. Daily 10am–5pm. MAP PP.38–39, POCKET MAP C3

Fun, tourist-oriented clothes store selling all manner of T-shirts, caps, hats, woollen sweaters and the like, as well as Iceland souvenirs.

THE VIKING

Hafnarstræti 1–3 ☎ 551 1250, ⓦ theviking .is. Mon, Thurs & Fri 9am–9pm, Tues & Wed 9am–8pm, Sat 9am–10pm, Sun 10am–8pm. MAP PP.38–39, POCKET MAP C3

From pens to fridge magnets, sheepskin rugs to woollen sweaters, this popular souvenir shop's got it covered. There's also a collection of books about Iceland, plus postcards.

Cafés and restaurants

BÆJARINS BEZTU PYLSUR

Tryggvagata 1 ☎ 511 1566, ⓦ bbp.is. Mon–Thurs & Sun 10am–1am, Fri & Sat 10am–4.30am. MAP PP.38–39, POCKET MAP D3

Hidden away on a patch of waste ground between Tryggvagata and Hafnarstræti, *Bæjarins* is a local institution, having opened in 1937. From a small kiosk they serve up the Nordic classic: a *pylsa* (hot dog; 400kr), with lashings of fried onion and artery-clogging remoulade sauce. Be prepared to queue.

BÆJARINS BEZTU PYLSUR

FISH MARKET

Aðalstræti 12 ☎ 578 8877, ⓦ fishmarket.is.
Mon–Fri 11.30am–2pm & 6–11.30pm, Sat &
Sun 6–11.30pm. MAP PP.38–39, POCKET MAP C4
Smart, stylish restaurant heavy
on fake greenery and specializing in dishes given an Asian
twist – try the salted cod with
lime (4800kr) or the grilled
pork ribs with star anise and
cardamom (2800kr). All
produce is bought direct from
Icelandic fishermen and farmers.

GRILLHÚSIÐ

Tryggvagata 20 ☎ 562 3456, ⓦ grillhusid.is.
Mon–Thurs & Sun 11.30am–10pm, Fri & Sat
11am–11pm. MAP PP.38–39, POCKET MAP C3
Popular and informal grill
restaurant, especially popular
at weekends, decked out to
resemble an American diner.
The menu runs to pricey steaks,
but it's best for its burgers
(from 1790kr) or fish and
chips (2370kr).

HORNIÐ

Hafnarstræti 15 ☎ 551 3340, ⓦ hornid.is. Daily
11am–11.30pm. MAP PP.38–39, POCKET MAP D3
Another classic Reykjavík
restaurant that's stood the test
of time – this one has been
here since 1979 and is popular
for the excellent pizzas (around

2390kr) and pasta (around
2450kr). They also do a good
range of meat and fish dishes,
with a daily fish special
(3650kr) and a succulent lamb
fillet (4990kr).

ICELANDIC FISH & CHIPS

Tryggvagata 11 ☎ 511 1118, ⓦ fishandchips.is.
Mon–Thurs 11.30am–9.30pm, Fri–Sun
11.30am–10pm. MAP PP.38–39, POCKET MAP B2
Proper sit-down restaurant in
the Volcano House (see p.40)
serving exactly what you'd
expect from the name. The type
of fish available varies daily,
but the sides on offer
don't – whatever you choose,
simply add fries, onion rings or
salad, or other garnishes such
as delicious home-made dips.

KRUA THAI

Tryggvagata 14 ☎ 561 0039, ⓦ kruathai.is.
Mon–Fri 11.30am–9.30pm, Sat noon–9.30pm,
Sun 5–9.30pm. MAP PP.38–39, POCKET MAP C2
This cosy, no-nonsense Thai
place offers exceptional value,
with a huge choice of
single-dish meals – green curry,
pad thai and the like – for
around 1760kr. Servings are
generous and prices include
rice. At lunchtime, a portion of
three different set dishes with
rice goes for a mere 1450kr.

REYKJAVÍK FISH RESTAURANT

Tryggvagata 8 ☎ 578 5656, ⓦ reykjavikfish.is.
Daily 11am–10.30pm. MAP PP.38–39, POCKET MAP C2

Another of Reykjavík's restaurants catering to the current craze for British-style fish and chips – here you can choose tangy sauces to go with them such as mango chilli or lemon pepper and dill. There's also a great smoked salmon salad, fish soup and delicious Arctic char with potato salad.

Bars

DOLLY

Hafnarstræti 4 ☎ 571 9222. Wed & Thurs
8pm–1am, Fri & Sat 8pm–4.30am. MAP PP.38–39,
POCKET MAP C3

This cool and rather intimate little lounge bar, full of battered furniture, plays a range of hip-hop and electronica. It's a popular place with a young crowd who come here to drink (seriously) and dance (unsteadily).

DUBLINER

Naustin 1 ☎ 527 3232, ⓦ dubliner.is. Mon &
Tues 4pm–midnight, Wed 4pm–1am, Thurs
3pm–1am, Fri 3pm–4.30am, Sat 1pm–4.30am,
Sun 1pm–midnight. MAP PP.38–39, POCKET MAP C3

Iceland's first-ever Irish pub still draws in the crowds. It's always a good choice for an evening pint, and there's a reasonable selection of whiskeys, plus live music (often Irish folk and R&B) every night of the week.

FREDERIKSEN ALE HOUSE

Hafnarstræti 5 ☎ 571 0055, ⓦ frederiksen.is.
Mon–Thurs & Sun noon–1am, Fri & Sat
noon–5am. MAP PP.38–39, POCKET MAP C3

This well-located pub is busy at any time of day. There's a decent selection of draught and bottled beers, including Víking classic, Thule and stout. The expert staff are also adept at knocking up wicked cocktails.

GAUKURINN

Tryggvagata 22 ☎ 781 7273, ⓦ gaukurinn.is.
Wed & Thurs 9pm–1am, Fri & Sat 9pm–4.30am.
MAP PP.38–39, POCKET MAP C3

Long-established, though recently renovated, this live music venue and bar has been drawing the crowds since even before beer was legalized in 1989. You'll find a mix of live music, karaoke, open mic nights and pub quiz events (see the website for details).

ICELANDIC FISH & CHIPS

The harbour

North of Geirsgata, the busy main road which runs parallel to the shoreline, lies Reykjavík harbour, built around reclaimed land – the beach where vessels once landed their foreign goods is now well inland from here. Street names in this area, such as Ægisgata (ocean street) and Öldugata (wave street), reflect the importance of the sea to the city, and a stroll along the dockside demonstrates Iceland's dependence on the Atlantic, with fishing trawlers being checked over and prepared for their next battle against the waves, and plastic crates of ice-packed cod awaiting transportation to village stores around the country. Keep an eye out, too, for the black whaling ships, each with a red "H" painted on its funnel (*hvalur* is Icelandic for "whale"), which are usually moored here. Ironically, the harbour is also the departure point for whale-watching and puffin-spotting tours.

SAGA MUSEUM

Grandagarður 2 ☎ 511 1517, Ⓦ sagamuseum .is. Daily 10am–6pm. 2000kr. MAP P.45, POCKET MAP A1

Housed in a former fish storehouse on the western edge of the harbour, the excellent Saga Museum is Iceland's answer to Madame Tussauds.

The expertly crafted wax models of characters from the sagas and their reconstructed farms and homes are employed, superbly, to depict medieval Icelandic life, often a misunderstood period in the country's history. A visit here will give you a sense of what life must have been like in Iceland centuries ago, and all

SAGA MUSEUM

The harbour

| 0 | metres | 200 |
| 0 | yards | 200 |

SHOP

Epal   1

CAFÉS & RESTAURANTS

Búllan   5
Café Haiti   7
Fish & Chips
  Vagninn   4
Kaffivagninn   1
MAR   8
Matur og Drykkur   3
Sægreifinn   6
Sjávarbarinn   2

BARS

Forrétta Barinn   2
SKY Lounge & Bar   3
Slippbarinn   1

Whales of Iceland

Saga Museum

Sjóminjasafn

Vesturhöfn

Reykjavík Harbour

Whale-watching, puffin-spotting and sea-angling tours

Old Harbour

Harpa

GEIRSGATA

TRYGGVAGATA

INGOLFSTORG SQUARE

ACCOMMODATION

Icelandair Reykjavík Marina   1
Reykjavík Downtown Hostel   2

the big names are here: Snorri (see p.98), who even breathes deeply as he ponders; Eirík the Red; and Leifur Eiríksson (see p.65) and his sister Freyðis, the latter portrayed slicing off her breast as a solitary stand against the natives of Vínland who, after killing one of her compatriots, turned on her – according to the sagas, Freyðis's actions saw her aggressors immediately take flight. An informative audioguide (included in the admission fee) explains a little about each of the characters on display – and also about the smells of the period, which have been synthetically reproduced inside, too.

SJÓMINJASAFN

Grandagarður 8 ☎ 411 6300, ⓦ maritime museum.is. Daily 10am–5pm. Museum 1400kr; Óðinn 1200kr; 2000kr for both. MAP P.45, POCKET MAP M1

Given Iceland's prominence as a seafaring nation, Reykjavík's Maritime Museum is a disappointment. A ragtag collection of old fishing hooks, dried fish and model boats, this tired exhibition of fisheries through the ages is dull in the extreme. The only saving grace is the former coastguard vessel, *Óðinn*, moored in the dock outside (daily guided tours at 1pm, 2pm & 3pm). Built in Denmark in 1959, the ship patrolled Iceland's territorial waters in the North Atlantic until 2006, taking part in all three cod wars with the UK. The cutters used to slice through the nets of British trawlers are displayed on *Óðinn*'s rear deck. Note that you can peep at *Óðinn* without entering the museum: it's visible from the rear of the site.

WHALES OF ICELAND

Fiskislóð 23 ⓦ whalesoficeland.is. Daily:
May–Sept 9am–9pm; Oct–April 9am–6pm.
2900kr. MAP P.45, POCKET MAP M1

This creative new museum has
drawn plenty of criticism over
its entry price, but it offers a
unique opportunity (in
Iceland) to appreciate the full
magnificence of these massive
marine mammals, whose true
bulk is hidden beneath the
surface of the water. Located in
a vast purpose-built warehouse,
the museum contains 23
life-size models suspended
from the ceiling; walking
among them gives an amazing
perspective on their sheer size.
Exceptionally well executed,
with steel skeletons and silicon
skins, the models were made in
China and shipped to Iceland
in sections – the blue whale, for
example, is as long as a tennis
court. Virtually every species
found in Icelandic waters is
represented: the sperm whale,
humpback, minke and even
beluga are all here.

HARPA

Austurbakki 2 ⓦ harpa.is. Daily 8am–
midnight. Free. MAP P.45, POCKET MAP E2

A striking new addition to
the Reykjavík skyline, the
eye-catching Harpa opera
house had a difficult birth. At
the time of the economic crash
in 2008, the structure was
barely half built and a host of
politicians and decision-makers
called for the scheme to be
scrapped, arguing that Iceland
shouldn't be building something
so opulent in the circumstances.
Amid much derision, however,
the project went ahead and has
produced one of the city's most
memorable buildings. Taking its
cue from Iceland's unusual
geological forms, Harpa's
exterior is composed of

HARPA

hexagonal glass cubes, designed to resemble the basalt columns of lava seen all over the country; during the dark winter months, light shows illuminate the glass panels, producing ingenious displays of colour and shapes. The main feature of the airy interior is the classic, shoebox-shaped concert hall, **Eldborg**, with seating for up to 1800. The country's premier venue for concerts and theatre productions, Harpa is also home to the Icelandic symphony orchestra and national opera. Visitors are free to wander around the building at leisure, and the café on the ground floor makes an agreeable place to watch the comings and goings of the harbour through the hexagonal windows.

Whale watching, puffin spotting and sea angling

Whale watching

Tours leave throughout the year (up to twelve departures daily depending on the season), sailing for Faxaflói bay north of Reykjavík. You're most likely to encounter minke whales, white-beaked dolphins and harbour porpoises, though orcas, humpbacks and dolphins can also be spotted; blue, fin and sei whales will also occasionally put in an appearance. You can check the success rate of sightings on previous trips on the company websites below, and should you fail to see any whales or dolphins on your tour, the companies will offer you a free trip, which can be taken at any time within the next two years.

Puffin spotting

Between mid-May and mid-August (after which the birds head out to sea for the winter months), there are twice-daily tours around the islands of Lundey and Akurey, where puffins gather to breed in the summer. Although it's not possible to go ashore, you'll have a great view of the cliffs and grassy slopes which make up the islands' sides, and the burrows where the puffins live. Remember, though, that puffin numbers have fallen in recent years due to a lack of the birds' main source of food, the sand eel. It's a good idea to ask about the tide conditions before choosing a departure because the boats get closer to the islands on a high tide.

Sea angling

Between May and August, sea-angling tours depart three times daily from the harbour, giving you a chance to try out your deep-sea skills – you get to keep anything you catch. Catfish, cod, haddock, mackerel and pollack are the most commonly landed, and you can barbecue your catch on board, should you choose. Alternatively, you can take it to the *MAR* restaurant (see p.48), where they will cook it for you (included in the trip cost).

Operators

Recommended operators include Elding on Ægisgarður (☎ 519 5000, ⓦelding.is), who offer whale watching (9000kr), puffin spotting (5500kr) and sea angling (12,500kr); and Special Tours, also on Ægisgarður (☎ 560 8800, ⓦspecialtours.is), who offer the same activities: whale watching (9000kr); puffin spotting (5000kr); and sea angling (11,500kr).

Shops

EPAL

Inside Harpa concert hall, Austurbakki 2
☎ 515 7733, ⓦ epal.is. Mon–Fri 10am–6pm,
Sat 11am–4pm, Sun noon–4pm. MAP P.45,
POCKET MAP E2

A good stop if you're in the
market for items from
Scandinavia's top design houses
such as Normann Copenhagen,
Design House Stockholm,
Marimekko and Iittala.

Cafés and restaurants

BÚLLAN

Geirsgata 1 ☎ 511 1888, ⓦ bullan.is. Daily
11.30am–9pm. MAP P.45, POCKET MAP B2

This unimpressive little 1950s
concrete bunker of a building
at the harbour feels like an
American diner inside – and
they serve nothing but burgers
(from 1030kr) and excellent
fries. Expect to queue.

CAFÉ HAITI

Geirsgata 7c ☎ 588 8484, ⓦ cafehaiti.is.
Mon–Thurs 8am–10pm, Fri 8am–11pm,
Sat 9am–11pm, Sun 9am–8pm. MAP P.45,
POCKET MAP C2

Run by the effervescent Elda,
who grew up and lived in Haiti
until meeting her late Icelandic
husband, this funky café offers
home-roasted coffee as well as
some delicious soups. It holds
frequent art exhibitions and
live music events, too.

FISH & CHIPS VAGNINN

On the seafront at the junction of Rastargata
and Hlésgata ☎ 840 4100, ⓦ fishandchips
vagninn.is. Daily 11am–9pm. MAP P.45,
POCKET MAP B1

Owned by three Icelandic
families who have all lived and
worked in the UK in the
seafood business, this mobile
trailer serves deliciously fresh,
British-style takeaway fish and
chips – the fish is Icelandic, the
chips are from Dutch potatoes
and the trailer is from Leeds in
West Yorkshire. There are a few
alfresco tables and chairs, too.

KAFFIVAGNINN

Grandagarður 10 ☎ 551 5932, ⓦ kaffivagninn
.is. Mon–Fri 7.30am–6pm, Sat & Sun
9.30am–6pm. MAP P.45, POCKET MAP M1

Claiming to be the oldest eating
establishment in Reykjavík, this
fishermen's café down in the
harbour is great for breakfast
(served till 11am) or weekend
brunch (11am–3pm). They also
specialize in Danish-style open
sandwiches as well as serving a
wide range of cakes.

MAR

Geirsgata 9 ☎ 519 5050, ⓦ marrestaurant.com.
Daily 11.30am–11pm. MAP P.45, POCKET MAP C2

Named after the Latin word for
"sea", MAR is a top-notch fish
restaurant offering a creative
menu which combines fresh
Icelandic seafood with the
flavours of the Mediterranean
and Caribbean: marinated
scallops in a coconut and lime
sauce; pan-fried cod with
mustard, sesame seeds and a
tomato and lime salsa; mussel
soup with pickled carrot. Mains
around 3300kr.

MATUR OG DRYKKUR

Grandagarður 2 ☎ 571 8877,
ⓦ maturogdrykkur.is. Tues–Sat
11.30am–11.30pm, Sun & Mon
11.30am–5.30pm. MAP P.45, POCKET MAP A1

Inside the Saga Museum
building, this inventive new
restaurant, plainly decked out
with a concrete floor and
wooden tables, has a truly
unusual menu, featuring
everything from an entire
baked cod's head, with throat
muscles in batter on the side

MATUR OG DRYKKUR

(3490kr), to cod liver on caraway crackers served with cranberries (1490kr).

SÆGREIFINN

Geirsgata 8 ☎ 553 1500, ⓦ saegreifinn.is.
Daily 11.30am–11pm. MAP P.45, POCKET MAP B2
This harbourside fishmonger-cum-restaurant is a favourite haunt of locals who know the superlative lobster soup (1350kr) is the best in town. There's plenty of fresh fish on the menu, too, such as halibut, which is served on skewers. It's also the place to come for minke whale steaks (1850kr), if your conscience allows.

SJÁVARBARINN

Grandagarður 9 ☎ 517 3131, ⓦ sjavarbarinn.is.
Mon–Fri 9am–9pm, Sat 10am–10pm, Sun 4–10pm. MAP P.45, POCKET MAP M1
Handy for the Saga and Maritime museums, this little fish place really comes into its own at lunchtime when there's a seafood buffet for just 1790kr, featuring a range of fish dishes, a bowl of soup, and coffee.

Bars

FORRÉTTA BARINN

Nýlendugata 14 ☎ 517 1800, ⓦ forrettabarinn
.is. Mon–Fri 4pm–midnight, Sat & Sun noon–midnight. MAP P.45, POCKET MAP B2

With a lengthy happy hour (daily 4–8pm), this funky bar serves a good range of beers from Icelandic brewery, Kaldi, as well as international brands like Stella, Hoegaarden, Pilsner Urquell and Leffe. During happy hour you can get a beer here from 500kr.

SKY LOUNGE & BAR

Inside Centerhotel Arnarhvoll, Ingólfsstræti 1
☎ 595 8545, ⓦ skylounge.is. Daily
11.30am–midnight. MAP P.45, POCKET MAP F3
Sip a cocktail at this rooftop bar – part of the *Centerhotel* – while enjoying superb views out towards the opera house and all the way to Mount Esja. They run a daily happy hour (5–7pm) and rustle up well-prepared canapés and more substantial bar snacks, such as BLT and club sandwiches.

SLIPPBARINN

Mýrargata 2–8 ☎ 560 8080, ⓦ slippbarinn.is.
Daily 5pm–late. MAP P.45, POCKET MAP B1
This swanky and sophisticated place, inside the *Icelandair Reykjavík Marina* hotel (see p.116), has to be the most novel location for a bar in the whole of town – right beside the slipway where the ships come in to be repainted and repaired.

SÆGREIFINN

Tjörnin and around

From the harbour, Pósthússtræti leads south past the bars and restaurants of Tryggvagata, Hafnarstræti and Austurstræti to Tjörnin, which is invariably translated into English as "the lake" or "the pond". *Tjörn* and its genitive form of *tjarnar* are actually old Viking words, still used in northern English dialects as "tarn" to denote a mountain lake. Originally a lagoon inside the reef that once occupied the spot where Hafnarstræti now runs, this sizeable body of water, roughly a couple of square kilometres in size, is populated by forty to fifty varieties of birds – including the notorious arctic tern, known for their dive-bombing attacks on passers-by, which are found at the lake's quieter southern end. The precise numbers of the lake's bird population are charted on noticeboards stationed at several points along the bank.

RÁÐHÚSIÐ

Tjarnargata 11. Mon–Fri 8am–7pm, Sat & Sun noon–6pm. Free. MAP P.51, POCKET MAP C5

Occupying prime position on the northern edge of Tjörnin is Ráðhúsið (City Hall). Opened in 1992, it's a showpiece of Nordic design, a modernist rectangular structure of steel, glass and chrome that actually sits on the lake itself. Inside, in addition to the city's administration offices, is a small café and, in one of the small exhibition areas, a fabulous self-standing **topographical model** of Iceland that gives an excellent impression of the country's unforgiving geography – you

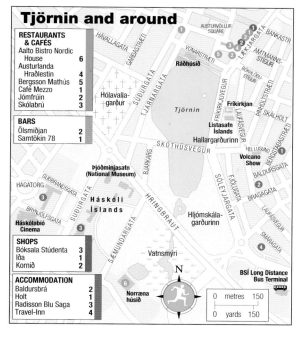

Tjörnin and around

RESTAURANTS & CAFÉS	
Aalto Bistro Nordic House	6
Austurlanda Hraðlestin	4
Bergsson Mathús	5
Café Mezzo	1
Jómfrúin	2
Skólabrú	3

BARS	
Ölsmiðjan	2
Samtökin 78	1

SHOPS	
Bóksala Stúdenta	3
Iða	1
Kornið	2

ACCOMMODATION	
Baldursbrá	2
Holt	1
Radisson Blu Saga	3
Travel-Inn	4

can marvel at the sheer size of the Vatnajökull glacier in the southeast (as big as the English county of Yorkshire) and the table mountains of the West Fjords, and gain instant respect for the people who live amid such challenging landscapes.

SUÐURGATA

One of the best views of Reykjavík can be had from Suðurgata, a street running parallel to Tjörnin's western shore; to get there from the City Hall, walk west along Vonarstræti, crossing Tjarnargata. Suðurgata is lined with tidy little dwellings, but from it you can see across the lake to the city centre's suburban houses, whose corrugated-iron roofs, ranging in colour from a pallid two-tone green to bright blues

and reds, have been carefully maintained by their owners – the familiar picture-postcard view of Reykjavík.

VIEW FROM SUÐURGATA

ÞJÓÐMINJASAFN

Suðurgata 41 ☎ 530 2200, 🌐 thjodminjasafn
.is. 10am–5pm: May to mid-Sept daily;
mid-Sept to April Tues–Sun. 1500kr. MAP P.51,
POCKET MAP A7

By far the most engaging part of the National Museum, Þjóðminjasafn, is the **first floor**, which covers the period from 800 to 1600; the video presentation within the "Origin of Icelanders" exhibition, devoted to the early Viking period and the use of DNA testing, is particularly good. Recent genetic research has shown that whereas around eighty percent of today's Icelanders are of Nordic origin, sixty-two percent of the early Viking-era women originated from the British Isles; the conclusion reached is that the first settlers sailed from Scandinavia to Iceland, stopping off at the British Isles along the way to marry.

Another prime exhibit is the small human figure, about the size of a thumb and made of bronze, which is thought to be over a thousand years old and to portray either the Norse god Þór or Christ. More spectacular is the carved church door from Valþjófsstaður in Fljótsdalur, dating from around 1200, and depicting the medieval tale *Le Chevalier au Lion*: it features an ancient warrior on horseback slugging it out with an unruly dragon. The Danish authorities finally gave up the treasure in 1930 and returned the door to Iceland, together with a host of medieval manuscripts. Check out, too, the impressive Romanesque-style carved Madonna dating from around 1200, which hails from northern Iceland and is displayed within the "Medieval church" section.

The **second floor** of the museum, devoted to the period from 1600 onwards, canters through key events in Icelandic history such as the Trade Monopoly (1602–1787) and the birth of the republic. The displays conclude with a revolving airport-style conveyor belt laden with twentieth-century appliances and knick-knacks, featuring everything from a Björk LP to a milking machine.

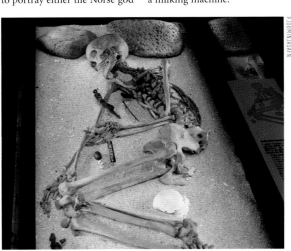

ÞJÓÐMINJASAFN

LISTASAFN ÍSLANDS

Fríkirkjuvegur 7 ☎ 515 9600, ⓦ listasafn.is.
Tues–Sun: June–Aug 10am–5pm; Sept–May
11am–5pm. 1000kr. MAP P.51, POCKET MAP D6

A few minutes' walk north from the National Museum down Sóleyjargata, which runs along the eastern side of Tjörnin, passing the offices of the Icelandic president at the corner of Skothúsvegur, is the **Fríkirkjan** (Free Lutheran Church). The best feature of this simple wooden structure, painted whitish grey, is its high green roof and tall tower, useful as a landmark to guide you to the neighbouring former ice house, known as **Herðubreið**. Once a storage place for massive chunks of ice, hewn in winter from the frozen lake and used to preserve fish stocks, the building has been enlarged and completely redesigned, and houses Listasafn Íslands (the National Gallery of Iceland). Icelandic art may lack worldwide recognition, but all the significant names are to be found here, including Erró, Jón Stefánsson, Ásgrímur Jónsson, Guðmundur Þorsteinsson and Einar

LISTASAFN ÍSLANDS

Hákonarson – though, disappointingly, lack of space (there are only three small exhibition rooms containing barely twenty or so paintings each) means that the works can only be shown in strictly rationed portions from the museum's enormous stock of around eleven thousand pieces of art. You can get an idea of the paintings not on display by glancing through the postcards sold at reception.

All aboard!

Next stop, Reykjavík Central Station... As curious as it sounds in a country prone to any number of earth tremors and eruptions, plans to build a **railway line** from central Reykjavík to Keflavík airport are being seriously considered. Due to its inhospitable terrain and low population, Iceland is one of the few European countries not to have a rail network of any kind. However, if plans get the go-ahead, that will all change, with a high-speed track laid across the lavafields of the Reykjanes Peninsula, drastically reducing the journey time to the international airport and cutting exhaust emissions. Although no site has been officially earmarked for a train station in Reykjavík, the favourite remains the rather ramshackle BSÍ bus terminal, which could then be transformed into a modern transport interchange fit for a capital city. Currently, the bus station is owned by Reykjavík Excursions who operate the Flybus to Keflavík airport.

Shops

BÓKSALA STÚDENTA

Sæmundurgata 4 ☏ 570 0777, Ⓦ boksala.is. Mon–Fri 9am–5pm. MAP P.51, POCKET MAP M3

This bookshop, which belongs to the university, is probably the best-stocked in the whole of Iceland. It holds a wide range of teach-yourself-Icelandic texts, as well as glossy coffee-table books about the country.

IÐA

Lækjargata 2a ☏ 511 5001, Ⓦ ida.is. Daily 9am–10pm. MAP P.51, POCKET MAP D5

Engaging gift store selling a range of tasteful souvenirs from Iceland. Also doubles as a mini-bookshop with a selection of travel guides and other books about the country.

KORNIÐ

Lækjargata 4 ☏ 564 1800, Ⓦ kornid.is. Mon–Fri 7am–5.30pm, Sat & Sun 7am–5pm. MAP P.51, POCKET MAP D4

This popular bakery-cum-café, a mere stone's throw from Tjörnin, specializes in fresh breads, other baked goods and good coffee, and offers outdoor seating in summer along the pavement of Lækjargata.

Cafés and restaurants

AALTO BISTRO NORDIC HOUSE

Sturlugata 5 ☏ 551 0200, Ⓦ nordice.is. Mon–Wed & Sun 11am–5pm, Thurs–Sat 11am–9pm. MAP P.51, POCKET MAP M3

Located in the Nordic House, a Nordic cultural centre, this new bistro operates under TV chef Sveinn Kjartansson, who mixes Icelandic and central European cuisines: how about hot-smoked catfish on a citrus salad with wild angelica mayonnaise, or some lavender and orange cake topped with *skyr* (Icelandic yoghurt)?

AUSTURLANDA HRAÐLESTIN

Lækjargata 8 ☏ 578 3838, Ⓦ hradlestin.is. Mon–Thurs 11am–10pm, Fri 11am–11pm, Sat & Sun 5–11pm. MAP P.51, POCKET MAP D4

Sporting the most un-Icelandic name you could imagine, "Oriental Express Train" boasts that its menu is full of genuine Indian dishes, though its offerings are tempered to the more conservative Icelandic palate. A curry goes for around 2495kr – note that they're not shy of food colourings.

AALTO BISTRO

BERGSSON MATHÚS

Templarasund 3 ☎ 571 1822, ⓦ bergsson.is. Mon–Fri 7am–7pm, Sat & Sun 7am–5pm. MAP P.51, POCKET MAP C4

This snug bistro serves home-made dishes such as spinach lasagne and chilli con carne (1390–2290kr). Breakfasts and brunches featuring the likes of Spanish ham, eggs, and yoghurt with muesli and berry jam are top-notch.

CAFÉ MEZZO

Lækjargata 2a ☎ 571 3150, ⓦ mezzo.is. Daily 9am–10pm. MAP P.51, POCKET MAP D4

Airy first-floor café located above the Iða store (see opposite) that's popular with a young crowd. There's a good choice of speciality coffees on offer and, at lunchtime, the Caesar salad always hits the spot. Check out the changing display of art or photography exhibitions which adorn the walls.

JÓMFRÚIN

Lækjargata 4 ☎ 551 0100, ⓦ jomfruin.is. Daily 11am–6pm. MAP P.51, POCKET MAP D4

Jómfrúin is a popular Danish-influenced place specializing in *smørrebrød* (open rye sandwiches), priced at 1800–3300kr. Pick your toppings from a range which includes smoked salmon, caviar, asparagus, smoked eel and scrambled egg. Fried plaice (2200kr) is the house speciality.

SKÓLABRÚ

Pósthússtræti 17 ☎ 511 1690, ⓦ skolabru.is. Mon–Thurs 5.30–10pm, Fri & Sat 5.30–11pm. MAP P.51, POCKET MAP D4

A sophisticated, fine-dining place offering the likes of seawolf with roast vegetables served in a mango, chilli and ginger sauce, and Parmesan-crusted chicken with tomatoes and mashed potatoes. Three-course set menus start at 6600kr.

SKÓLABRÚ

Bars

ÖLSMIÐJAN

Lækjargata 10 ☎ 578 0440. Mon–Thurs & Sun 3pm–1am, Fri & Sat 3pm–5am. MAP P.51, POCKET MAP D4

Perhaps not the most sumptuous of Reykjavík's bars, but then people come here for the prices, not the fantastic interior design: you can get a beer for roughly the same price charged by other places during their happy hours. Long weekend opening hours complete the deal.

SAMTÖKIN 78

Suðurgata 3 ☎ 552 7878, ⓦ samtokin78.is. Thurs 8–11pm. MAP P.51, POCKET MAP C4

Once a week, Reykjavík's gay community gathers here at the new premises of the national LGBT association, Samtökin 78, for an evening of chat, discussion and the chance to socialize over a beer or a coffee. The community centre is also open to non-Icelanders and you'll be sure of a warm welcome.

Bankastræti and around

Northeast of the National Gallery, Lækjartorg Square is bounded to the east by Bankastræti and by Lækjargata to the south. Lækjargata once marked the eastern boundary of the town and Tjörnin still empties into the sea through a small brook which now runs under the road here (*lækjar* comes from *lækur*, meaning "brook") – occasionally, when there's an exceptionally high tide, seawater gushes back along the brook, pouring into Tjörnin. The cluster of old timber buildings up on the small hill immediately south of Bankastræti is known as Bernhöftsstofan and, following extensive renovation, they now house a couple of chichi fish restaurants (see p.62). Named after Tönnies Daniel Bernhöft, a Dane who ran a nearby bakery, they're flanked to the north by one of Iceland's most important buildings, Stjórnarráðshúsið.

MENNTASKÓLINN AND STJÓRNARRÁÐSHÚSIÐ

Both closed to the public. MAP PP.58–59. POCKET MAP D4–5

Reykjavík's elegant old Grammar School, **Menntaskólinn**, built in 1844, once had to be accessed by a bridge over the brook. It also housed the Alþingi before the completion of the current Alþingishúsið (see p.32) in nearby Austurvöllur Square. Just north of Bankastræti, the small, unobtrusive white building at the foot of Arnahóll hill (see opposite) is, in fact, one of the seats of power in Iceland: **Stjórnarráðshúsið** (Government House) contains the cramped working quarters of the prime minister. It's one of the city's oldest-surviving buildings, built in 1761–71 as a prison.

MENNTASKÓLINN

ARNAHÓLL

MAP PP.58–59, POCKET MAP E3

Up on Arnahóll, the grassy mound behind the Icelandic prime minister's offices, a statue of Ingólfur Arnarson, Reykjavík's first settler, surveys his domain; with his back turned on the National Theatre, and the government ministries to his right, he looks out to the ocean that brought him here over eleven centuries ago. Experts believe this is the most likely spot where the pillars of Ingólfur's high seat – a sort of Viking-era throne – finally washed up; according to *Landnámabók*, they were found "by Arnarhvál below the heath".

ARNAHÓLL

HVERFISGATA

MAP PP.58–59, POCKET MAP E4–K6

One of central Reykjavík's main thoroughfares, Hverfisgata has always played second fiddle to its more glitzy neighbour to the south, Laugavegur. True, it has fewer bars, restaurants and shops than Laugavegur, but a recent makeover has improved things greatly – new pavements have been laid and the whole street has been spruced up. Hverfisgata is at its grandest at its southern end – it's here you'll find the elegant **Danish Embassy** at no. 29 and also the former National Library, now the Safnahús museum, just a few doors down.

Magnússon's manuscripts

Despite so many of Iceland's sagas and histories being written down by medieval monks for purposes of posterity, there existed no suitable means of protecting them from the country's damp climate, and within a few centuries these unique artefacts were rotting away. Enter **Árni Magnússon** (1663–1730), humanist, antiquarian and professor at the University of Copenhagen, who attempted to ensure the preservation of as many of the manuscripts as possible by sending them to Denmark for safekeeping. Although he completed his task in 1720, eight years later many of them went up in flames in the Great Fire of Copenhagen, and Árni died a heartbroken man fifteen months later, never having accepted his failure to rescue the manuscripts, despite braving the flames himself.

In 1961, legislation was passed in Denmark decreeing that manuscripts composed or translated by Icelanders should be returned, but it took a further ruling by the Danish Supreme Court, in March 1971, to get things moving. Finally, however, in April of that year, a Danish naval frigate carried the first texts, *Konungsbók Eddukvæða* and *Flateyjarbók*, across the Atlantic into Reykjavík, to be met by crowds bearing signs reading "handritin heim" ("the manuscripts are home") and waving Icelandic flags. A new building, the **Hús íslenskra fræða** (House of Icelandic Studies), is currently under construction near the National Museum on Suðurgata to house the collection.

Bankastræti and around

0 metres 100
0 yards 100

FAXAGATA
KALKOFNSVEGUR
KALKOFNSVEGUR
SÆBRAUT
SÆBRAUT
SKÚLAGATA
SÖLVHÓLSGATA
INGÓLFSSTRÆTI
Arnarhóll
LINDARGATA
SKÚLAGATA SUND
AUSTURSTRÆTI
LÆKARTORG SQUARE
HVERFISGATA
HVERFISGATA
Safnahús
Hverfisgalleri
Þjóðleikhúsið
KLAPPARSTÍGUR
Stjórnarráðshúsið
BANKASTRÆTI
VEGHÚSASTÍGUR
HVERFISGATA
Dómkirkjan
AMTMANNSSTÍGUR
SKÓLABRÚ SUND
SMIÐJUSTÍGUR
LÆKJARGATA
Menntaskólinn
LAUGAVEGUR
KLAPPARSTÍGUR
VONARSTRÆTI
BÖKHLÖÐUSTÍGUR
ÞINGHOLTSSTRÆTI
INGÓLFSSTRÆTI
HALLVEIGARSTÍGUR
VEGAMÓTASTÍGUR
FRAKKASTÍGUR
N
GRETTISGATA
SPÍTALASTÍGUR
BERGSTAÐASTRÆTI
SKÓLAVÖRÐUSTÍGUR
NJÁLSGATA
ÓÐINSGATA
TÝSGATA
LOKASTÍGUR
BJARNAST
FREYJUGATA
BRAGAGATA
KÁRASTÍGUR
FRAKKASTÍGUR

SHOPS
66° North — 1
Dogma — 3
Handprjónasamband Íslands — 4
Timberland — 2

SAFNAHÚS

Hverfisgata 15 ☎ 530 2210, ⓦ culturehouse.is. Tues–Sun 10am–5pm. 1200kr. MAP PP.58–59, POCKET MAP E4

Sadly, the Safnahús (Culture House) has lost its way. Until recently the home of a remarkable exhibition about Iceland's medieval manuscripts, today the museum has been subject to an amateurish makeover and contains nothing more than a hotchpotch of seemingly random items from the country's past. While individual pieces may impress, the overriding impression left to the visitor by the muddled exhibition (known as "Points of View") is one of disappointment – this could, and should, be so much better.

Though the **ground floor** is predominantly given over to religious art, it also, confusingly, contains more contemporary items such as a photographic portrait of former Icelandic president, Vigdís Finnbogadóttir, plonked alongside an ornate seventeenth-century tapestry and a sculpture of Mary from the church in Vatnsfjörður, dated around 1400–1500. It's a juxtaposition which doesn't work. Elsewhere on the ground floor, however, do look out for the various versions of *Jónsbók*, a grouping of ancient legal texts which date from 1281; most impressive is the modern copy of a text from 1363, replete with ornately decorated initial letters.

The **first and second floors** contain a mishmash of exhibits – and, once again, the ad hoc combination of items is quite arbitrary: for example,

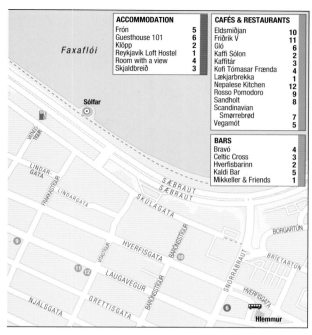

ACCOMMODATION	
Frón	5
Guesthouse 101	6
Klöpp	2
Reykjavík Loft Hostel	1
Room with a view	4
Skjaldbreið	3

CAFÉS & RESTAURANTS	
Eldsmiðjan	10
Friðrik V	11
Gló	6
Kaffi Sólon	2
Kaffitár	3
Kofi Tómasar Frænda	4
Lækjarbrekka	1
Nepalese Kitchen	12
Rosso Pomodoro	9
Sandholt	8
Scandinavian Smørrebrød	7
Vegamót	5

BARS	
Bravó	4
Celtic Cross	3
Hverfisbarinn	2
Kaldi Bar	5
Mikkeller & Friends	1

a magnificent altar piece from the church at Grenjaðarstaður, dating from 1766, rubs shoulders with a garish piece of modern art from 1948, *Big sister and little brother* by Kristján Davíðsson. That said, it's worth seeking out the stuffed great auk, hidden away in a small alcove off the main staircase leading to the top floor. Bought at auction in London in 1971, it's thought the bird was killed at Hólmsberg on the Reykjanes Peninsula (see p.84) – the last two great auks in the world were bludgeoned to death on June 3, 1844 on the nearby island of Eldey.

LAUGAVEGUR

MAP PP.58-59, POCKET MAP G5-K6

From Lækjartorg, turn right into the short Bankastræti and on, up the small hill, into Laugavegur ("hot spring road"), the route once taken by local washerwomen to the springs in Laugardalur. This is Iceland's major commercial artery, holding the main shops and a fair sprinkling of cafés, bars and restaurants. Not surprisingly, therefore, on Friday and Saturday evenings in summer it's bumper to bumper with cars, horns blaring and with well-oiled revellers hanging out of the windows. However, during the summer months, large sections of Laugavegur are accessible only to pedestrians and cyclists – a decision by the City Council that has been warmly welcomed by the majority of the city's population who have long complained that this was one of the city's worst bottlenecks.

HANDPRJÓNASAMBAND ÍSLANDS

Shops

66° NORTH

Bankastræti 9 ☎ 535 6680, ⓦ 66north.com.
Mon–Sat 9am–7pm, Sun 10am–6pm.
MAP PP.58–59, POCKET MAP E4

Renowned for good-quality (if
expensive) clothes which are
guaranteed to keep the worst of
the Icelandic weather at bay –
there's more than a grain of
truth in their slogan: "Keeping
Iceland warm since 1926".

DOGMA

Laugavegur 32 ☎ 562 6600, ⓦ dogma.is.
Mon–Thurs 10am–6pm, Fri 10am–6.30pm, Sat
10am–5pm. MAP PP.58–59, POCKET MAP G5

If you're after a T-shirt as a
souvenir of your stay in
Reykjavík, chances are you'll
find a contender here. They
stock the classic *ég tala ekki
íslensku* ("I don't speak
Icelandic") range, too.

HANDPRJÓNASAMBAND
ÍSLANDS

Laugavegur 53B and Skólavörðustígur 19 ☎ 552
1890, ⓦ handknit.is. Laugavegur branch: Mon–Fri
9am–10pm, Sat 9am–6pm, Sun 10am–6pm;
Skólavörðustígur branch: Mon–Fri 9am–7pm, Sat
10am–5pm. MAP PP.58–59, POCKET MAP F5

The Icelandic handknitting
association sells an astounding
number of home-made
woollens. Each item has been
produced by a knitter in the
Reykjavík area, and quality is
high – reckon on around
15,000–20,000kr for a decent
sweater. Tax-free shopping
available (see p.133).

TIMBERLAND

Laugavegur 6 ☎ 533 2290, ⓦ timberland.is.
Mon–Sat 10am–6pm, Sun noon–5pm.
MAP PP.58–59, POCKET MAP E4

This has to be one of the
company's cutest stores – a
gorgeous pitch-roofed timber
building from 1871 at the foot
of Laugavegur. They offer
tax-free shopping here, too.

Cafés

KAFFI SÓLON

Bankastræti 7a ☎ 562 3232. Mon–Thurs
11am–11.30pm, Fri & Sat 11am–1am, Sun
11am–11pm. MAP PP.58–59, POCKET MAP E4

Decked out in contemporary
Icelandic design, this is one of
Reykjavík's most popular cafés
and serves a good range of light
meals (upwards of 1990kr) –
from beef teriyaki and burgers
to deep-fried camembert and
salads – as well as heartier
mains (around 3990kr).

KAFFITÁR

Bankastræti 8 ☎ 420 2732, ⓦ kaffitar.is. Mon–Sat 7.30am–6pm, Sun 9am–5pm. MAP PP.58–59, POCKET MAP E4

The Icelandic version of *Starbucks*, but with far better coffee, made from expertly blended beans (available as a brand in supermarkets). The usual run of cakes and muffins is on offer, too, plus good croissants.

KOFI TÓMASAR FRÆNDA

Laugavegur 2 ☎ 551 1855. Mon–Thurs 10am–1am, Fri & Sat 10am–5am, Sun 10am–midnight. MAP PP.58–59, POCKET MAP E4

Also known simply as *Kofinn*, trendy young Reykjavíkers flock to this chilled place to loll around on the comfortable couches, chat, drink coffee and work on their poetry. Its prime position on Laugavegur is also great for people-watching.

SANDHOLT

Laugavegur 36 ☎ 551 3524, ⓦ sandholt.is. Mon–Wed 6.30am–8pm, Thurs–Sat 6.30am–9pm. MAP PP.58–59, POCKET MAP G5

The best café-cum-bakery in town with good coffee and excellent strawberry tarts, cinnamon swirls, flans, fresh sandwiches and handmade chocolates. Also serves breakfast including fresh croissants, muesli and *skyr*.

KAFFI SÓLON

FRIÐRIK V

Laugavegur 60 ☎ 461 5775, ⓦ fridriku.is. Tues–Sat 5.30pm–late. MAP PP.58–59, POCKET MAP H6

Run by the ebullient Friðrik, who trained at London's *River Café*, the tasting menu here lets you sample new Nordic cooking at its most inventive, with Icelandic herbs and flavours allied perfectly to the very best of Mediterranean influences. The three-course tasting menu is 8400kr; the five-course version 10,400kr.

Restaurants

ELDSMIÐJAN

Laugavegur 81 ☎ 562 3838, ⓦ eldsmidjan.is. Daily 11am–11pm. MAP PP.58–59, POCKET MAP J6

Boasting a prime location on the main drag, *Eldsmiðjan* serves the best pizzas in Reykjavík, made in an oven that burns Icelandic birchwood. There's also a takeaway service available. A twelve-incher starts at 2995kr.

FRIÐRIK V

GLÓ

GLÓ

Laugavegur 20B ☎ 553 1111, Ⓦ glo.is.
Mon–Fri 11am–9pm, Sat & Sun
11.30am–9pm. MAP PP.58–59, POCKET MAP F5
Unusually decorated with
slices of birch trunks, this
popular vegetarian place
serves up the likes of parsley
root soup with hummus
(1250kr) and nut stew
(1990kr). The emphasis is on
fresh produce, much of it
served uncooked. Also sells a
wide range of fresh juices.

LÆKJARBREKKA

Bankastræti 2 ☎ 551 4430, Ⓦ laekjarbrekka
.is. Daily 11.30am–11pm. MAP PP.58–59,
POCKET MAP D4
Housed in an old wooden
building with period
furnishings, *Lækjarbrekka*
offers a refined atmosphere and
fabulous seafood – including
a mouthwatering seafood
(7900kr). The "Icelandic feast"
(9500kr) includes fermented
shark, cured lamb, minke
whale, dried fish, lamb, cream
of langoustine soup and *skyr*
mousse with blueberry sorbet.

NEPALESE KITCHEN

Laugavegur 60A ☎ 517 7795, Ⓦ nepalese
kitchen.is. Mon–Sat 5.30–11pm, Sun
5.30–10pm. MAP PP.58–59, POCKET MAP H6

This Nepalese restaurant has a
deserved reputation for serving
some seriously tasty dishes
from the Indian subcontinent:
mains, such as Nepalese
chicken masala and any
number of lamb and vegetarian
specialities, start at around
2990kr. You can get a fifteen
percent discount if you're
ordering takeaway.

ROSSO POMODORO

Laugavegur 40 ☎ 561 0500, Ⓦ rossopomodoro
.is. Mon–Thurs 11.30am–10pm, Fri & Sat
11.30am–11pm, Sun 5–10pm. MAP PP.58–59,
POCKET MAP G5

LÆKJARBREKKA

A genuinely good southern Italian restaurant, drawing inspiration from Neapolitan cuisine. Pizzas and pasta dishes go for around 2990kr, salads start at 1790kr and grilled chicken with Parma ham, mozzarella and red wine sauce, for example, is 4390kr.

SCANDINAVIAN SMØRREBRØD

Laugavegur 22A ☎ 578 4888, ⓦ scandinavian .is. Mon–Thurs 11.30am–1pm, Fri & Sat 11.30am–11pm. MAP PP.58–59. POCKET MAP F5

Under new ownership, this place (despite its name) serves Icelandic rather than Scandinavian specialities, such as reindeer pâté, lobster soup and various lamb dishes (mains around 3500kr). There's a range of open sandwiches, too.

VEGAMÓT

Vegamótastígur 4 ☎ 511 3040, ⓦ vegamot.is. Mon–Thurs & Sun 11.30am–1am, Fri & Sat 11.30am–4am. MAP PP.58–59. POCKET MAP F5

A favourite hangout for Reykjavík's trendy young things, who come here for the good-value burgers (2590kr), salads (2490kr), Mexican specials (2590kr), and the excellent weekend brunch (Sat & Sun 11am–4pm; from 2390kr).

Bars

BRAVÓ

Laugavegur 22 ☎ 770 1517. Mon–Thurs & Sun 7pm–1am, Fri & Sat 7pm–4.30am. MAP PP.58–59, POCKET MAP F5

In various guises, this spot has been one of Reykjavík's most popular bars for years, and is a great place to start the evening. The music policy is varied, embracing everything from electro to indie and classic hits.

CELTIC CROSS

Hverfisgata 26 ☎ 571 1033. Mon–Thurs & Sun 11.30am–1am, Fri & Sat 11.30am–4am. MAP PP.58–59. POCKET MAP F4

Best of the Brit/Irish pubs in town; the beer is the same (Guinness and lager), but the atmosphere is livelier – especially when rock and R&B bands fire up at weekends. There's decent pub grub, too.

HVERFISBARINN

Hverfisgata 20 ☎ 776 0171. Fri & Sat 9pm–3am. MAP PP.58–59. POCKET MAP F4

The bar and club here on the corner of Hverfisgata and Smiðjustígur has always been popular with Reykjavík's in-crowd. Hverfisbarinn is now back in business after a makeover and is still attracting anyone who's young and beautiful – or at least who thinks they are. There are often long queues to get in.

KALDI BAR

Laugavegur 20B ☎ 581 2200, ⓦ kaldibar.com. Mon–Thurs & Sun noon–1am, Fri & Sat noon–3am. MAP PP.58–59. POCKET MAP F5

Kaldi Bar serves up any number of beers from the Kaldi microbrewery in Árskógssandur near Akureyri. They play low background music, so if you're looking for a place to chat over a drink, it's a sound choice. Note that it's often packed.

MIKKELLER & FRIENDS

Hverfisgata 12 ☎ 437 0203, ⓦ mikkeller.dk /mikkeller-friends-reykjavik. Mon–Thurs & Sun 4pm–midnight, Fri & Sat 2pm–1am. MAP PP.58–59. POCKET MAP E4

With twenty beers on tap, all from microbreweries, this great little top-floor bar is a beer drinker's heaven. It's cosy and snug inside, and a really good place to kick the evening off with a drink or two.

Hallgrímskirkja and around

From the western end of Laugavegur, Skólavörðustígur streaks steeply upwards to the largest church in the country, the magnificent Hallgrímskirkja, a magnet for all tourists visiting Reykjavík. With its burgeoning number of shops and restaurants, the street is fast becoming a rival to Laugavegur, albeit in shorter form. Thanks to its hilltop vantage point, meanwhile, the church enjoys some of the best views of central Reykjavík of anywhere in the city. From Hallgrímskirkja, it's an easy stroll back down the hill, perhaps detouring via the excellent swimming pool, Sundhöllin (see p.129), towards Hlemmur, Reykjavík's main bus interchange, and on to the seafront. Here, there are sweeping views out over Faxaflói bay across to Mount Esja in the distance.

HALLGRÍMSKIRKJA

Skólavörðuholt ☎ 510 1000, ⦿ hallgrimskirkja .is. Daily: June–Aug 9am–9pm; Sept–May 9am–5pm. Free; viewing platform 800kr.
MAP PP.66–67, POCKET MAP G7

The Reykjavík skyline is dominated by this modern concrete structure, with its neatly composed, space-shuttle-like form. Work began on the church – named after the renowned seventeenth-century religious poet Hallgrímur Pétursson – immediately after World War II, but was only completed in 1986, the slow progress due to the task being carried out by a family firm comprising one man and his son. The work of state architect Guðjón Samúelsson, the church's unusual design – not least its 73m steeple – has divided the city over the years, although locals have grown to accept rather than love it since its consecration. Most people rave about the **pipe organ** inside, the only decoration in an otherwise completely bare, Gothic-style shell; measuring a whopping 15m in height and possessing over five thousand pipes, it really has to be heard (during services) to be believed.

The tower has a **viewing platform**, accessed by a lift from just within the main door, giving stunning panoramic views across Reykjavík; note that it's open to the elements.

LEIFUR EIRÍKSSON STATUE

MAP PP.66–67, POCKET MAP G7

With his back to the church and his gaze firmly planted on

Time is of the essence

Spend any time in Reykjavík and you'll soon understand that the city lives at the mercy of the elements. Rain and snow storms can appear as if from nowhere and howling winds, tearing straight in off the sea, can cut through all but the most robust of outdoor gear. Understand that and it's easy to see why no two public clocks in Reykjavík tell the same time. Exposure to the sea, altitude and general meteorological mayhem cause radically diverse wind conditions in different parts of the city. At the top of Hallgrímskirkja tower, for example, the wind is so strong that the hands on the clock are frequently blown off course. It's something Icelanders don't give a second thought to, of course, but it's not unusual to spot baffled tourists double-checking their watches to make sure of the correct time.

Vínland, the imposing statue of **Leifur Eiríksson**, the Icelandic explorer who is considered by many to have discovered North America, was donated by the US in 1930 to mark the Icelandic parliament's thousandth birthday. This is one of the highest parts of Reykjavík, and on a clear day there are great **views** out over the surrounding houses adorned with multicoloured corrugated-iron facades.

LISTASAFN EINARS JÓNSSONAR

Eiríksgata 3 ☎ 551 3797, ⓦ lej.is. June to mid-Sept Tues–Sun 2–5pm; mid-Sept to Nov & Feb–May Sat & Sun 2–5pm. 1000kr. MAP PP.66-67, POCKET MAP F7

The heroic form of Leifur Eiríksson is found in several other statues around the city, many of them the work of Einar Jónsson (1874–1954), who is remembered by this museum, housed in a pebble-dash building to the right of Hallgrímskirkja. Einar lived here in an increasingly reclusive manner until his death in 1954; a specially constructed group of rooms, connected by slim corridors and a spiral staircase, takes the visitor through a chronological survey of Einar's career. His style of sculpture varies widely, though is often influenced by his spiritual beliefs and by Icelandic mythology. If the

museum is closed, peek into the **garden** at the rear, where several examples of Einar's work are displayed; his most visible work, the statue of independence leader Jón Sigurðsson, stands in front of the Alþingishúsið (see p.32).

HIÐ ÍSLENZKA REÐASAFN

Laugavegur 116 ☎ 561 6663, ⓦ phallus.is. Daily 10am–6pm. 1250kr. MAP PP.66-67, POCKET MAP K6

The Hið Íslenzka Reðasafn (Phallological Museum) is easy to spot – just look for the bemused-looking tourists standing outside, not quite believing that this is, indeed, a museum dedicated to the penis. Visitors can ogle the members of around three hundred mammals, displayed in jars of formaldehyde and alcohol. It's now possible to size up a human specimen too, following the death of 95-year-old Páll Arason, who had pledged his manhood to the museum (be warned – it comes complete with long white wisps of pubic hair). And there's more: a misshapen foreskin removed in an emergency operation and a pair of human testicles are also on display. After that, you'll no doubt be ready for the plaster cast and photos of several former museum visitors, which leave little to the imagination.

CAFÉS & RESTAURANTS	
Café Babalú	3
Café Loki	6
Fish & More	4
Kaffifélagið	2
Kól	5
Mokka	1
Þrir Frakkar	7

| | 0 | metres | 150 | |
| | 0 | yards | 150 | |

SHOPS	
Frú Lauga	3
Geysir	2
Ostabúðin	1

SÓLFAR

Sæbraut. MAP PP.66–67, POCKET MAP H4

From Hlemmur it's just a couple of blocks north to the seafront where the striking *Sólfar* ("Sun Voyager") sculpture is worthy of your attention. This sleek contemporary portrayal of a Viking-age ship, made of shiny silver steel by Jón Gunnar Árnason (1931–89), sits elegantly atop the city shoreline and is fast becoming one of the most photographed of Reykjavík's

SÓLFAR

Hallgrímskirkja and around

Faxaflói

N

BARS
Bjórgarðurinn	2
Hlemmur Square	3
Kaffibarinn	1

ACCOMMODATION
Adam	7
Fosshótel Baron	1
Fosshótel Lind	8
Fosshótel Reykjavík	2
Hlemmur Square	4
Leifur Eiríksson	6
Luna	5
Óðinsvé	3

attractions. You'll find it on Sæbraut, the main road which runs along the shore, close to the junction with Frakkastígur.

HÖFÐI

Borgartún. Closed to the public. MAP PP.66–67, POCKET MAP P2

East of Sólar, it's a five-minute stroll back along Sæbraut to Höfði, a stocky white wooden structure built in 1909 in Jungendstil, which occupies a grassy square beside the shore, between Sæbraut and Borgartún. Originally home to the French consul, the house also played host to Winston Churchill in 1941 when he visited British forces stationed in Iceland. Although Höfði is best known as the location for the 1986 snap summit between Soviet President Mikhail Gorbachev and US President Ronald Reagan, Icelanders know it equally well for its resident ghost, said to be that of a young girl who poisoned herself after being found guilty of incest with her brother.

HÖFÐI

Shops

FRÚ LAUGA

Óðinsgata 1 ☎ 534 7185, Ⓦ frulauga.is.
Mon–Sat 11am–6pm. MAP PP.66–67, POCKET MAP F5

Farmers' market selling the
freshest of Icelandic fruit and
vegetables – from raspberries
to broccoli – delivered directly
to the shop every day from
across the country.

GEYSIR

Skólavörðustígur 16 ☎ 519 6000, Ⓦ geysir.com.
Daily 9am–10pm. MAP PP.66–67, POCKET MAP F5

This is the only place you
should consider buying a pure
wool Icelandic blanket – even
though you'll need to part with
around 17,800kr. The quality is
far superior to other shops and
tax-free shopping is available.

OSTABÚÐIN

Skólavörðustígur 8 ☎ 562 2272, Ⓦ ostabudin.
is. Mon–Thurs 10am–6pm, Fri 10am–6.30pm,
Sat 11am–4pm. MAP PP.66–67, POCKET MAP E5

Ostabúðin offers a great choice
of Icelandic cheeses, as well as
charcuterie and other
delicatessen items. Downstairs
there are also a few tables
where you can get a light lunch
– try the creamy fish soup.

GEYSIR

Cafés and restaurants

CAFÉ BABALÚ

Skólavörðustígur 22a ☎ 555 8845,
Ⓦ babalu.is. Daily 11am–11pm. MAP PP.66–67,
POCKET MAP F6

This quirky, bohemian café
occupies two floors of a
brightly painted yellow
building and is popular with
an alternative crowd. Their
cheesecake is heavenly.

CAFÉ LOKI

Lokastígur 28 ☎ 466 2828, Ⓦ loki.is. Mon–Sat
9am–9pm, Sun 11am–9pm. MAP PP.66–67,
POCKET MAP F7

Traditional Icelandic fare at
reasonable prices: meat soup
(1570kr), herring plate
(2200kr), sheep head jelly on
flatbread (1840kr) and *skyr*
(820kr). Great views of
Hallgrímskirkja from upstairs.

FISH & MORE

Skólavörðustígur 23 ☎ 571 1289. Daily
10am–9.30pm. MAP PP.66–67, POCKET MAP F6

Instead of battering and frying,
this fish restaurant steams the
catch and serves it with veggies
(2290kr); check the blackboard
to see what's fresh in that day.
There's often a deliciously tangy
fish soup, too (1590kr).

KAFFIFÉLAGIÐ

Skólavörðustígur 10 ☎ 520 8420,
Ⓦ kaffifelagid.is. Mon–Fri 10.30am–6pm, Sat
10am–4pm. MAP PP.66–67, POCKET MAP E5

Proudly boasting to be the
smallest café in the whole of
Iceland, this minuscule place
serves a range of different
coffees produced by the Italian
company, Ottolina, which has
been in operation since 1947.
Either drink in or take away;
ground coffee beans are also
available for purchase.

horse tenderloin with mushrooms (5750kr), *plokkfiskur* (fish and potato mash; 3600kr) and smoked guillemot (5190kr).

Bars

BJÓRGARÐURINN

Þórunnartún 1 ☎ 531 9013, ✆ bjorgardurinn .is. Daily 11.30am–midnight. MAP PP.66–67, POCKET MAP P2

Attached to the *Fosshótel*, the "Beer Garden" has an impressive range of beer both on tap and in bottles, including pilsner, stout, pale ale and brown ale. Happy hour is 5–7pm, when there are some great deals to be had. Don't miss the sausages in a brioche bun, either.

HLEMMUR SQUARE

Laugavegur 105 ☎ 415 1600, ✆ www .hlemmursquare.com/bistro-bar. Daily 3–10pm. MAP PP.66–67, POCKET MAP K6

The trendy bar inside the *Hlemmur Square* hostel (see p.119) should be your number one choice for happy hour (4–8pm), with beers priced at an amazing 600kr (there are several Icelandic ones on tap, as well as Tuborg), and even cocktails going for just 1000kr.

KAFFIBARINN

Bergstaðastræti 1 ☎ 551 1588. Mon–Thurs & Sun 5pm–1am, Fri & Sat 3pm–5am. MAP PP.66–67, POCKET MAP F5

With an unmistakable red corrugated-iron frontage emblazoned with the famous London underground logo, this tiny bar fancies itself as an arty hangout and trades on the rumour that Blur's Damon Albarn owns it, however unlikely. Be that as it may, it's still perhaps your best bet for a great night out in Reykjavík and is a legend on the scene.

KÓL

Skólavörðustígur 40 ☎ 517 7474, ✆ kolrestaurant.is. Mon–Thurs 11.30am–2pm & 5.30–10pm, Fri 11.30am–2pm & 5.30–11pm, Sat 5.30–11pm, Sun 5.30–10pm. MAP PP.66–67, POCKET MAP F6

This classy place is named after the *kól* (charcoal) over which they cook their meat: the grilled lamb sirloin with polenta, carrots and goat's cheese, for example, is delicious (4890kr). The fish – from charred salmon to plaice – is also tasty.

MOKKA

Skólavörðustígur 3a ☎ 552 1174. Daily: June–Aug 9am–9pm; Sept–May 9am–6.30pm. MAP PP.66–67, POCKET MAP E5

Reykjavík's oldest café opened in 1958, and was the first in the country to serve espresso and cappuccino to its curious clientele. A changing display of photographs adorn the walls, and there's a no-music policy.

ÞRIR FRAKKAR

Baldursgata 14 ☎ 552 3939, ✆ 3frakkar.com. Mon–Thurs 11.30am–2.30pm & 6–10pm, Fri 11.30am–2.30pm & 6–10.30pm, Sat & Sun 6–10.30pm. MAP PP.66–67, POCKET MAP E7

Strange name ("Three Overcoats") for this backstreet, French-style bistro with definite leanings towards traditional Icelandic game:

Öskjuhlíð and around

The wooded hill of Öskjuhlíð (60m above sea level) affords spectacular views of the city, and is a popular recreation area for Reykjavíkers, who flock here to explore the paths that crisscross its verdant slopes. Öskjuhlíð has, in fact, only been wooded since 1950, when a forestation programme began after soil erosion had left it barren and desolate. A plot of land on the hill's southern side, near the inlet of Fossvogur and the Fossvogskirkjugarður cemetery, has recently been earmarked as the location for a temple to the Æsir, the heathen gods of Viking times, though building work has yet to commence.

PERLAN

Öskjuhlíð ☎ 562 0200, 🌐 perlan.is. Daily 10am–9pm. Free. MAP P.71, POCKET MAP N4

If you arrive in Reykjavík from Keflavík airport, it's hard to miss the space-age-looking grey container tanks that sit at the top of the wooded hill, Öskjuhlíð. Each is capable of holding four thousand litres of water at 80°C for use in the capital's homes, offices and swimming pools; it's also from here that water has traditionally been pumped, via a network of specially constructed pipes, underneath Reykjavík's pavements to keep them ice- and snow-free during winter. The whole thing is topped by a **revolving restaurant**, Perlan, which is a truly spectacular place for dinner – if your wallet can take the strain.

Even if you're not eating here, you can still enjoy a 360-degree **panoramic view** of the entire city: simply take the lift to the fourth floor and step outside. On a clear day you can see all the way to the Snæfellsjökull glacier at the tip of the Snæfellsnes peninsula, as well as the entirety of Reykjavík. Before leaving, make sure you see the artificial indoor **geyser simulator** that erupts every few minutes from the basement, shooting a powerful jet of water all the way to the fourth floor: it's a good taste of what's to come if you're heading out to the real thing at Geysir (see p.94).

PERLAN

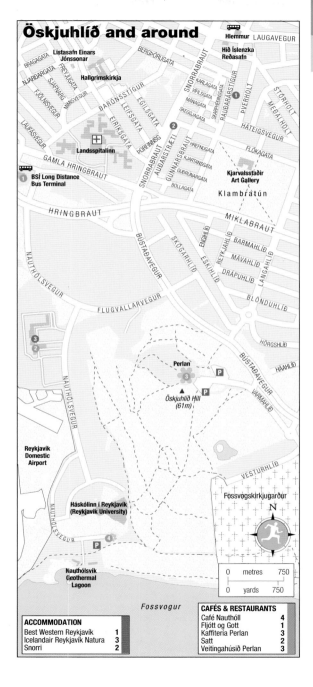

Öskjuhlíð and around

Listasafn Einars Jónssonar

Hallgrímskirkja

Landsspítalinn

BSÍ Long Distance Bus Terminal

Hlemmur · LAUGAVEGUR

Hið Íslenzka Reðasafn

Kjarvalsstaðir Art Gallery

Klambratún

Perlan

Öskjuhlíð Hill (61m)

Reykjavík Domestic Airport

Háskólinn í Reykjavík (Reykjavik University)

Nauthólsvík Geothermal Lagoon

Fossvogskirkjugarðar

N

Fossvogur

| 0 | metres | 750 |
| 0 | yards | 750 |

ACCOMMODATION

Best Western Reykjavik	1
Icelandair Reykjavik Natura	3
Snorri	2

CAFÉS & RESTAURANTS

Café Nauthóll	4
Fljótt og Gott	1
Kaffiteria Perlan	3
Satt	2
Veitingahúsið Perlan	3

ÖSKJUHLÍÐ AND AROUND

NAUTHÓLSVÍK GEOTHERMAL LAGOON

Nauthólsvegur ☎ 551 3177, 🌐 nautholsvik.is.
Site open 24hr; changing facilities mid-May to
mid-Aug daily 10am–7pm (free); rest of the year
Mon–Fri 11am–1pm (Mon & Wed also 5–7pm),
Sat 11am–3pm. 500kr. MAP P.71, POCKET MAP N4

At the southern end of
Öskjuhlíð, close to the
Reykjavík Sailing Club, there's
an artificial beach of bright
yellow sand, known as Ylströnd,
where it's possible to swim in an
enclosed **seawater lagoon** (the
water temperature is generally
15–19°C). There are also two
hot pots on the beach (around
38°C), one of which is built into
the sand. In the winter, the
temperature in the lagoon is a
more invigorating 4-6°C.

Nauthólsvík is one of the best
places in the city to relax and
take the alfresco waters. Not
only does the site offer great
views of the southern coastline,
but it's also unfenced and open
to the surrounding countryside, meaning you can simply
come and go as you please.
Note that there are no lockers
in the changing rooms
themselves, just open baskets
for your clothes, though it is
possible to store valuables for
200kr – ask at the service

centre. Remember, as at other
Icelandic pools, you must
thoroughly shower naked,
without a swimming costume,
before entering the hot pots.

KJARVALSSTAÐIR

Flókagata 24 ☎ 517 1290, 🌐 artmuseum.is.
Daily 10am–5pm. 1400kr. MAP P.71, POCKET MAP N3

Its surroundings of birch trees
and pleasant grassy expanses
cannot hide the fact that the
Kjarvalsstaðir art gallery is an
ugly 1960s-style concrete
structure – even if the interior
is surprisingly bright and airy.
Part of the Reykjavík Art
Museum, Kjarvalsstaðir is
devoted to the work of Iceland's
most celebrated artist, Jóhannes
Sveinsson Kjarval (1885–1972).
After working on a fishing
trawler during his youth,
Jóhannes moved abroad to
study art, spending time in
London, Copenhagen, France
and Italy, but it was only after
his return to Iceland in 1940
that he travelled widely in his
own country, drawing on the
raw beauty he saw around him
for the quasi-abstract
depictions of Icelandic
landscapes which made him
one of the country's most
popular twentieth-century
painters. Painted in oils, much
of his work is a surreal fusion
of colour: his bizarre yet
pleasing *Krítik* ("Critique")
from 1946–7, a melee of icy
blues, whites and greys
measuring a whopping 4m in
length and 2m in height, is the
centrepiece of the exhibition,
portraying a naked man
jauntily bending over to expose
his testicles while catching a
fish, watched over, rather oddly,
by a number of Norse warriors.
The museum is divided into
two halls – the east one shows
Jóhannes's work, while the west
hall is dedicated to touring
temporary exhibitions.

KJARVALSSTAÐIR

Bars and restaurants

CAFÉ NAUTHÓLL

Nauthólsvegur 106 ☎ 599 6660, ⓦ nautholl
.is. Daily 11am–10pm. MAP P.71, POCKET MAP N4

This classy, airy bistro has
large windows overlooking
Fossvogur bay and serves a
good selection of tapas-style
nibbles during the day and
more substantial mains after
5pm. Also does a tempting
Sunday brunch (3150kr).

FLJÓTT OG GOTT

Inside the BSÍ bus terminal, Vatnsmýrarvegur
10 ☎ 552 1288, ⓦ fljottoggott.is. Daily
7.30am–9pm. MAP P.71, POCKET MAP N3

This keenly priced cafeteria
inside the BSÍ bus station is
more agreeable than you might
expect, serving a selection of
burgers and hot dogs, as well as
traditional Icelandic dishes.

KAFFITERÍA PERLAN

Inside the Perlan building, Öskjuhlíð
☎ 562 0200, ⓦ perlan.is. Daily 10am–9pm.
MAP P.71, POCKET MAP N4

For soups, sandwiches and light
salads, as well as a choice of
cakes and Italian ice cream, the
views from the café inside

CAFÉ NAUTHÓLL

Perlan are just as amazing as
those from the more upmarket
restaurant (see below), though
at a fraction of the cost.

SATT

Inside Icelandair Hótel Natura,
Nauthólsvegur 52 ☎ 444 4050,
ⓦ sattrestaurant.com. Daily 11am–10pm.
MAP P.71, POCKET MAP N3

Complete with a terrace for
sunny days, *Satt*, at the
Icelandair Natura hotel (see
p.120), offers a good-value
weekday lunch buffet (11.30am–
2pm), and a weekend brunch
deal (same times).

VEITINGAHÚSIÐ PERLAN

Inside the Perlan building, Öskjuhlíð ☎ 562
0200, ⓦ perlan.is. Daily 6.30pm–late. MAP P.71,
POCKET MAP N4

Located on the top floor of
the *Perlan* building and turning
one full circle every two hours,
a dinner here really is
something to remember – the
views and the food at this
top-notch, rotating restaurant
and bar are exquisite. Naturally,
none of this comes cheap;
reckon on 9350kr for a
four-course menu, and
upwards of 4700kr for a
main course of fish or
mountain lamb.

KAFFITERÍA PERLAN

Laugardalur and around

After rambling through central Reykjavík for a good couple of kilometres, Laugavegur comes to an end at the junction with the main north–south artery, Kringlumýrarbraut. Beyond here, Suðurlandsbraut marks the southern reaches of Laugardalur valley, hemmed in between the low hills of Grensás to the south and the northerly Laugarás, just behind Sundahöfn harbour, whose Þvottalaugarnar springs have been known since the time of the Settlement as a source of hot water for washing. The springs are still here, the spot commemorated by the Ásmundur Sveinsson statue, Þvottakonan (*The Washerwoman*), while the area is also home to Iceland's premier sports ground; an indoor sporting and concert venue; the HI youth hostel and campsite; and the country's largest swimming pool.

LAUGARDALSVÖLLUR AND LAUGARDALSHÖLL

MAP P.75, POCKET MAP P2

Open-air **Laugardalsvöllur** is the country's main sports stadium, hosting all of Iceland's international football and athletics fixtures. The largest attendance here was in 2004 for a friendly football match between Iceland and Italy, when over twenty thousand people packed into the ground to see the game – a staggering seven percent of the entire Icelandic population. Just to the south, across Engjavegur, **Laugardalshöll** hosts international indoor sporting events such as handball, volleyball and basketball. It is also the country's biggest concert venue, holding up to eleven thousand people. Should Iceland ever manage to win the Eurovision Song Contest (the dream of all Icelanders), Laugardalshöll would be the most likely choice

Swimming etiquette in Iceland

One of the best things about a trip to Reykjavík is the chance to swim outdoors in the city's geothermally heated swimming pools, whose water usually hovers around 23–25°C, and to loll in divinely warm **hot pots**, which tend to vary between 35 and 39°C. Since water in both the pools and the hot pots doesn't contain chlorine, strict rules are in place to ensure that bathers do not contaminate the water. Firstly, you must leave your outdoor shoes on the racks provided at the entrance to the changing room. Then, having undressed, you must **shower naked**, without a swimming costume, washing your body thoroughly with the soap provided in the areas marked on the multilingual signs posted up in the shower rooms: feet, hair, underarms, groin and bottom. Duty attendants will not hesitate to berate you should they spot you breaking the rules. Squeaky clean, you can now enjoy Iceland's best natural resource.

Laugardalur and around

of venue; Iceland came second in both 1999 and 2009.

LAUGARDALSLAUG

Sundlaugavegur ☎ 411 5100, ☍ itr.is. Mon–Fri 6.30am–10pm, Sat & Sun 8am–10pm. Entry 650kr. MAP P.75, POCKET MAP P2

Since opening in 1968, the swimming complex Laugardalslaug has become a Reykjavík institution. It is the biggest in Iceland and features a 50m outdoor pool, a smaller children's pool and paddling pool, two waterslides, numerous hot pots, a steam sauna, gym and mini-golf.

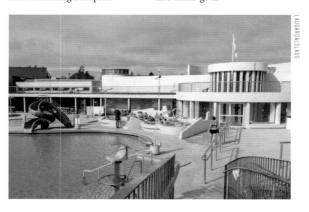

LAUGARDALSLAUG

ÁSMUNDARSAFN

Sigtún ⓦ artmuseum.is. Daily: May–Sept 10am–5pm; Oct–April 1–5pm. 1400kr. MAP P.75, POCKET MAP 02

If sculpture is your thing, you'll want to check out the domed Ásmundursafn, dedicated to the work of **Ásmundur Sveinsson** and part of the Reykjavík Art Museum. Sveinsson (1893–1982) was one of the pioneers of Icelandic sculpture, and his powerful, often provocative, work was inspired by his country's nature and literature. During the 1920s he studied in both Stockholm and Paris, returning to Iceland to develop his unique **sculptural Cubism**, a style infused with Icelandic myth and legend, which you can view here at his former home, which he designed and built with his own hands in 1942–50; he lived where the museum shop and reception are currently located.

The building is an uncommon shape for Reykjavík because, when Ásmundur planned it, he was experimenting with Mediterranean and North African themes, drawing particular inspiration from the domed houses common to Greece. The crescent-shaped building beyond reception contains examples of the sculptor's work, including several busts from his period of Greek influence. Note that the original of his most famous sculpture from 1926, **Sæmundur á selnum** (*Sæmundur on the Seal*), which shows one of the first Icelanders to receive a university education, the priest and historian Sæmundur Sigfússon (1056–1133), sitting astride a seal, psalter in hand, is not on display here; it stands outside the main university building on Suðurgata. You will, however, find a smaller version of the original in the museum grounds, where there are also lots of Ásmundur's other soft-edged, gently curved monuments to the ordinary working people of the country.

BOTANICAL GARDEN

No set hours. Free. MAP P.75, POCKET MAP 02-3

The green expanses beyond the sports ground contain the country's most impressive **botanical garden**. Barely ten minutes on foot from the Ásmundur Sveinsson sculpture museum, reached by walking east along Engjavegur, the botanical garden contains an extensive collection of native Icelandic flora, as well as thousands of imported plants and trees. This place is particularly popular with Icelandic families, who come here not only to enjoy the surroundings but also for the adjoining family park and small zoo (see opposite), which are a hit with children.

BOTANICAL GARDEN

HÚSDÝRAGARÐURINN AND FJÖLSKYLDUGARÐURINN

Hafrafell ⓦ mu.is. Daily: June–Aug 10am–6pm; Sept–May 10am–5pm. 800kr. Buses #2, #15 and #17 run from the city centre; get off at the Laugardalshöll stop. MAP P.75, POCKET MAP Q3

With children in tow, **Husdýragarðurinn zoo**, home to Icelandic mammals such as seals, foxes, mink and reindeer, makes a pleasant afternoon's visit. There's also a collection of fish caught in local rivers and lakes, which will keep younger visitors entertained. Once the attraction of the animals starts to wane, you can check out the surrounding **Fjölskyldugarðurin family park**, where there's a small duck lake complete with replica Viking longboat, a go-kart track, and other activities based loosely on a Viking theme, including a fort and an outlaw hideout.

KRINGLAN SHOPPING CENTRE

Kringlan 4–12 ☎ 517 9000, ⓦ kringlan.is. Mon–Wed 10am–6.30pm, Thurs 10am–9pm, Fri 10am–7pm, Sat 10am–6pm, Sun 1–6pm. A free shuttle bus operates here from outside the tourist office in Aðalstræti, where you'll find departure times. Alternatively, city buses #1, #3, #4 and #6 all come here. MAP P.75, POCKET MAP P3

The construction in 1987 of Kringlan shopping centre – the biggest in Reykjavík, with some 170 stores – took place amid concerns that it would lead to the closure of many shops in the city centre. Those fears turned out to be unfounded, as both Kringlan and the city centre have experienced an unprecedented boom in recent years, which shows no signs of ending. In addition to its stores, which feature well-known international names such as Diesel, Boss and Timberland as well as home-grown outlets, Kringlan also boasts a library,

KRINGLAN SHOPPING CENTRE

theatre, cinema and a branch of the state-owned alcohol monopoly, *vínbúðin*.

ÁRBÆJARSAFN

Kistuhylur 4 ☎ 411 6300, ⓦ arbaejarsafn.is. June–Aug daily 10am–5pm. 1400kr. POCKET MAP T2

The Árbæjarsafn open-air museum is a collection of turf-roofed and corrugated-iron buildings on the site of an ancient farm that was first mentioned in the sagas around the mid-1400s. The buildings and their contents record the changes that occurred as Iceland's economy switched from farming to fishing – the arrival of the fishing trawler heralded the beginning of the Icelandic industrial revolution – and Reykjavík's rapid expansion. The pretty **turf church** here, dating from 1842, is carefully moved to its present location from Skagafjörður on the north coast in 1960. Next to it, the farmhouse is dominated by an Ásmundur Sveinsson sculpture, *Woman Churning Milk*, illustrating an all-but-lost way of life.

VIÐEY

Ⓦ elding.is/videy. POCKET MAP Q1–R1

Reached by a short ferry ride from Sundahöfn harbour east of the city centre, and actually the top of an extinct volcano measuring barely 1.7 square kilometres, the island of Viðey has a rich heritage dating back to the time of the Settlement. You can see it from the mainland by taking a ten-minute walk north of the Laugardalur area along Dalbraut, which later mutates into Sundagarður. If you fancy a brisk stroll with views of the ocean and a bit of alfresco art thrown in, this is the place to come.

THE IMAGINE PEACE TOWER

Ⓦ imaginepeacetower.com. POCKET MAP Q1

To the left of the ferry landing on Viðey, in the opposite direction to the church, the unusual wishing-well structure you can see is the Imagine Peace Tower. Conceived in 2007 by Yoko Ono as a beacon to world peace and inscribed with the words "imagine peace" in 24 languages, the structure emits a powerful tower of light every night between October 9 (John Lennon's birthday) and December 8 (the anniversary of his death), illuminating the Reykjavík sky.

Shops

EYMUNDSSON

Kringlan shopping centre ☎ 540 2145, Ⓦ eymundsson.is. Mon–Wed 10am–6.30pm, Thurs 10am–9pm, Fri 10am–7pm, Sat 10am–6pm, Sun 1–6pm. MAP P.75, POCKET MAP D4

With a good selection of souvenirs, presents, maps and magazines, as well as coffee-table books about Iceland, Eymundsson is always worth a browse.

FINSKA BÚÐIN

Kringlan shopping centre ☎ 568 0606, Ⓦ finnskabudin.is. Mon–Wed 10am–6.30pm, Thurs 10am–9pm, Fri 10am–7pm, Sat 10am–6pm, Sun 1–6pm. MAP P.75, POCKET MAP P3

Finland's iconic designers Iittala and Marimekko are just some of the names you'll find inside this store, which sells stylish goods from Iceland's Nordic neighbour. There's an impressive selection of glasses, vases, bowls and fabrics, among other things.

VÍNBÚÐIN

Kringlan shopping centre ☎ 568 9060, Ⓦ vinbudin.is. Mon–Thurs & Sat 11am–6pm, Fri 11am–7pm. MAP P.75, POCKET MAP P3

Perfectly located for nipping in to buy a bottle of wine while out shopping at Kringlan, this outlet of *vínbúðin* is one of the busiest in the country. Knowledgeable staff are on hand to offer advice if you're looking for a specific tipple to match a meal.

Cafés and restaurants

BÆJARINS BEZTU PYLSUR

Kringlan shopping centre ☎ 511 1566, Ⓦ bbp.is. Mon–Wed 10am–7pm, Thurs 10am–9pm, Fri 10am–8pm, Sat 10am–6pm, Sun noon–6pm. MAP P.75, POCKET MAP P3

If you're in the market for a quick dine and dash, this long-standing favourite will hit the spot. *Bæjarins* claim that the combination they offer of hot dogs with a remoulade sauce is Iceland's national dish.

CAFÉ BLUE

Kringlan shopping centre ☎ 588 0300,
Ⓦ cafebleu.is. Mon–Wed, Fri & Sat
11am–8pm, Thurs 11am–9pm, Sun noon–8pm.
MAP P.75, POCKET MAP P3

Bright and breezy place with
an extensive menu featuring
pizzas (from 2290kr), burgers
(from 1790kr), sandwiches,
salads, pasta dishes (from
2390kr) and soups as well as a
few more substantial dishes
such as steaks, grilled lamb,
fish and chicken (3000–
4000kr).

ÍSLENSKA HAMBORGARAFABRIKKAN

Kringlan shopping centre ☎ 575 7575,
Ⓦ fabrikkan.is. Mon–Thurs & Sun
11am–10pm, Fri & Sat 11am–11pm. MAP P.75,
POCKET MAP P3

This popular restaurant has a
huge choice of burgers, both
beef (cooked medium rare)
and chicken, costing
1765–2495kr. Try the delicious
"Morthens", with bacon,
mushrooms, garlic and
Béarnaise sauce (2075kr).

HRAÐLESTIN

Kringlan shopping centre ☎ 578 3838,
Ⓦ hradlestin.is. Mon–Wed 11am–6.30pm, Thurs
11am–9pm, Fri 11am–7pm, Sat 11am–6pm, Sun
1–6pm. MAP P.75, POCKET MAP P3

Serving a range of Indian food,
including, curiously, an Indian
vegetarian pizza, this is the
place to come if you've tired of
the ubiquitous fish of the day
and lamb chops. The carrot
soup with ginger is good –
though remember that dishes
are geared towards the
conservative Icelandic palate.

JOE AND THE JUICE

Kringlan shopping centre ☎ 551 5757,
Ⓦ joeandthejuice.is. Mon–Wed 9.30am–7pm,
Thurs 9.30am–9pm, Fri 9.30am–7.30pm,
Sat 10am–6.30pm, Sun noon–6pm. MAP P.75,
POCKET MAP P3

This enterprising juice bar and
café blitzes just about
everything – from avocado to
ginger – into all manner of
delicious concoctions.

KAFFITÁR

Kringlan shopping centre ☎ 588 0440,
Ⓦ kaffitar.is. Mon–Wed 9.30am–6.30pm,
Thurs 9.30am–9pm, Fri 9.30am–7pm, Sat
9.30am–6pm, Sun 12.30–6pm. MAP P.75,
POCKET MAP P3

This chain opened in Kringlan
in 1995 and is one of
Reykjavíkers' favourite
coffeehouses. Grab a panini,
salad or home-made cake from
the café's own bakery – perfect
for taking a break from the
shopping marathon.

BÆJARINS BEZTU PYLSUR

Hafnarfjörður and around

Set amid an extensive lavafield, Hafnarfjörður, just 10km southwest of the capital, is as big as the centre of Reykjavík, although much more provincial in flavour. It's worth making the 25-minute bus ride out here to sample some real Viking food at the town's Viking village, Fjörukráin, and to learn more about the Icelanders' obsession with elves, dwarves and other spiritual beings – Hafnarfjörður is renowned across Iceland as having the country's greatest concentration of *huldufólk* ("hidden people").

HAFNARFJÖRÐUR MUSEUM

Vesturgata 8. June–Aug daily 11am–5pm; Sept–May Sat & Sun 11am–5pm. Free. MAP P.81, POCKET MAP A2–B2

A stone's throw from the northern end of Strandgata, one block to the north of the harbour, is Hafnarfjörður museum, housed in a wooden warehouse dating from the late 1800s and also known as Pakkhúsið. Inside is a passable if somewhat dull portrayal of Hafnarfjörður's life and times, featuring the likes of a stuffed goat and an old fishing boat.

SÍVERTSENS-HÚS

Vesturgata 6. June–Aug daily 11am–5pm; Sept–May Sat & Sun 11am–5pm. Free. MAP P.81, POCKET MAP A2

Next door to Hafnarfjörður museum stands Sívertsens-Hús, the town's oldest building, dating from 1803 and once the residence of local trader, boat builder and man-about-town Bjarni Sívertsen. It's now home to a folk museum, stuffed with how-we-used-to-live paraphernalia from the nineteenth century.

ÞRÍHNJÚKAHELLIR

☎ 519 5609, ⊚ insidethevolcano .com. Tours daily mid-May to Sept; 5–6hr including 40min inside the volcano, 39,000kr including return transport from Reykjavík.

About 20km southeast of Reykjavík, near the Bláfjöll ski area, lies Þríhnjúkahellir, an accessible, 4000-year-old subterranean magma chamber discovered in the 1970s which is like nowhere else in Iceland. There's little to see on the surface except for a small

HAFNARFJÖRÐUR HARBOUR

Hafnarfjörður and around

Víðistaðatún Park

Hellisgerði

Hafnarfjörður Museum & Sívertsens-Hús

Library

Bus to Reykjavík

Hafnarborg Arts Centre

Hamarinn

Hörðuvellir

Hamarkotslækur

Keflavík airport & Blue Lagoon

ACCOMMODATION	
Campsite	2
Helguhús	3
Hótel Víking	4
Lava Hostel	1

CAFÉS & RESTAURANTS	
Fjaran	6
Fjörugarðurinn	7
Gamla Vínhúsið	1
Gló	5
Silfur	4
Súfistinn	2
Tilveran	3

volcanic bump amid a landscape of moss and grass – but the scale below ground becomes clear once you've climbed into a **safety cage** and been lowered by crane into the 120m-deep space. Once you've touched down safely at the bottom, you're allowed to wander cautiously over the rough boulders and stones that carpet the floor of Þríhnjúka-hellir's 30m-wide chamber. Be sure to check out the walls, too, which are streaked in different colours left by molten minerals, all twisted and spiked by the forces. Normally a chamber such as this would fill with magma during an eruption and then solidify, but in Þríhnjúkahellir's case the molten rock drained out through tunnels, still visible at the sides of the cave floor. Note that you should wear warm

clothes and tough shoes or boots, as there is a 45-minute walk over rough ground at the beginning and end of the tour, to and from the volcano entrance. The tour ends with hot soup and bus transfer back to Reykjavík.

ÞRÍHNJÚKAHELLIR

HIDDEN PEOPLE

The hidden people

The street of Strandgata and neighbouring Austurgata in Hafnarfjörður are, according to Icelandic folklore, home to the town's population of hidden people – elves, dwarves and other spirits who live in entire families between the rocks that are dotted around the town centre. Apparently, elves are only visible to those with second sight, though a majority of Icelanders are quite prepared to admit they believe in them. In fact, an alarming number of new roads constructed across the country have been subject to minor detours around large rocks after workers attempted to move the boulders only to find that their diggers and earth movers broke down time and again in the process. Should you be keen to try out your second sight, occasional **tours** lasting a couple of hours leave from the tourist office at Strandgata 6 (Tues & Fri 2.30pm; 4500kr; ☎ 694 2785, ⊛ alfar.is); they weave their way through Hafnarfjörður, visiting the homes of the *huldufólk*, and are led by guide and storyteller Sigurbjörg Karlsdóttir.

Cafés and restaurants

FJARAN

Strandgata 55 ☎ 565 1213, ✆ fjorukrain.is.
Daily 6–10pm. MAP P.81
Located in the Viking village, this snug, wood-panelled restaurant is akin to a British country pub. It serves the same Viking delicacies as *Fjöru-garðurinn*, though is more refined (you'll get real plates rather than wooden platters).

FJÖRUGARÐURINN

Strandgata 55 ☎ 565 1213, ✆ fjorukrain.is.
Daily 6–10pm. MAP P.81
Designed to resemble a Viking longhouse, this atmospheric place, decked out with candles and heavy wooden tables, serves a full Viking dinner (9200kr) of seafood soup, shark, dried haddock and lamb shank, all washed down with beer and Black Death schnapps, and ending on *skyr* for dessert.

GAMLA VÍNHÚSIÐ

Vesturgata 4 ☎ 565 1130, ✆ gamlavinhusid
.is. Mon–Thurs 11.30am–9.30pm, Fri
11.30am–10.30pm, Sat 6–11.30pm, Sun
6–9.30pm. MAP P.81

The walls of this wooden-beamed place are lined with old wine bottles, creating a cosy atmosphere in which to savour baked cod fillet (3450kr), minke whale steak (2800kr), or just a house burger (1800kr). Lunch specials go for 1250kr.

GLÓ

Strandgata 34 ☎ 578 1111, ✆ glo.is.
Mon–Fri 11.30am–9pm, Sat & Sun
11.30am–5pm. MAP P.81
This great new restaurant in the Hafnarborg complex specializes in superb salads (1799kr) that feature the likes of mint, spinach and pomegranate in all sorts of zingy combinations.

SILFUR

Fjarðargata 13–15 ☎ 555 6996, ✆ silfur.wix
.com/silfur. Mon–Wed 10am–11pm, Thurs–Sat
10am–1am, Sun 11.30am–10pm. MAP P.81
This airy café in the Fjörður mall enjoys views over the harbour and serves burgers (from 1690kr), pasta (2290kr), plus fish and chips (1890kr).

SÚFISTINN

Strandgata 9 ☎ 565 3740, ✆ sufistinn.is.
Mon–Thurs 8.15am–11.30pm, Fri
8am–11.30pm, Sat 10am–11.30pm, Sun
11am–11.30pm. MAP P.81
Hafnarfjörður's main coffee-house, with outdoor seating in good weather. It's also a popular place for a beer of an evening.

TILVERAN

Linnetstígur 1 ☎ 565 5250,
✆ tilveranrestaurant.is. Mon–Thurs
11.30am–2pm & 6–9pm, Fri 11.30am–2pm &
6–10pm, Sat 6–10pm. MAP P.81
A justifiably popular seafood restaurant with daily lunch specials including soup, fish of the day and coffee for 2490kr; in the evening it's 2990kr for a succulent fish dish or 4490kr for meaty options.

The Reykjanes Peninsula

Southwest of Reykjavík city along the multi-lane Route 41, the Reykjanes Peninsula's rugged, lichen-covered lavafields jut out into the stormy waters of the Atlantic. It would be hard to imagine a wilder place so close to the capital, and yet here amid the seemingly bleak and lonely landscape are some real gems – not least the surreal splash of colour at the Blue Lagoon, Iceland's premier thermal spa. A couple of offbeat museums and a bizarre bridge in the middle of nowhere are worth a look in passing, but most of all it's the rocky, surf-streaked coastline, complete with associated birdlife, which rewards a day spent circuiting the peninsula: don't miss Selatangar's spooky ruins, the great auk monument and seething mud pools at Reykjanestá, nor the teeming bird colonies at Hafnaberg and Krýsuvíkurberg. Key sights such as the Blue Lagoon are easily reached on buses, but elsewhere you'll need your own vehicle or to join a tour.

THE BLUE LAGOON

Off Route 43 near Grindavík, around 45km from Reykjavík ⓦ bluelagoon.com. Daily Jan–May & Sept–Dec 10am–8pm, June–Aug 8am–10pm. 6500kr for lagoon; additional charges for spa, towels, meal packages etc; advance booking advised. MAP P.85, POCKET MAP S3

Forget the crush of tour buses, or the extravagant entry fee: your first sight of the Blue Lagoon, with its steaming, milky blue waters pooling amid a wilderness of black lava rubble, will make you glad you came to Iceland. Wade out into the shallow water (it's just about deep enough for swimming in places) or relax in the shallows, the heat seeping into your muscles; it's especially atmospheric on cold days, when a thick fog swirls and the waters feel even warmer.

The Blue Lagoon has its origins in local seawater, vaporized at the nearby **Svartsengi geothermal power station** and then fed – at a

Reykjanes Peninsula

N

0 miles 10
0 kilometres 15

Akranes
Hvalfjörður Tunnel
Grundarhvefi

Faxaflói

Mosfelsbær

REYKJAVIK
Hafnarfjörður
Elliðavatn

Garðskagi
Garður
Sandgerði
Hvalsne-skirkja
Keflavík
Stafnes
Keflavik International Airport
Vikingheimar
Njarðvík
Básendar
Hafnir

417

Þríhnjúkahellir

Reykjanes Peninsula

REYKJANES-FÓLKVANGUR

Kleifarvatn

427
Hlíðarvatn
Strandarkirkja

Blue Lagoon
Bridge Between Two Continents
Grindavik
427
Selatangar
Krýsuvíkurberg

Hafnaberg Cliffs
Reykjanestá
Gunnuhver Hot Springs
Saltfisksetur Íslands

ATLANTIC OCEAN

Eldey

RESTAURANTS
Bryggjan 4
Kaffi Duus 1
Lava Restaurant 3
Papa's 5
Pylsuvagn 6
T-Bær Café 7
Thai Keflavík 2

ACCOMMODATION
Northern Light Inn 1
Strandarkirkja Campsite 2

comfortable 38°C or so – into the lagoon. There's also a steam room, plus an artificial waterfall to stand under, while Icelanders scoop handfuls of silvery grey **silt** off the bottom of the lagoon to make facial mudpacks: it's said to cure skin disorders. Whatever the beneficial effects to your skin, your hair will take a real battering from the lagoon's mineral content; rub in plenty of conditioner as protection before bathing.

VIKINGHEIMAR (VIKING WORLD)

Víkingabraut 1, Njarðvík; heading west along Route 41, look for the cube-shaped building on the coast, about 5km before Keflavík town ⓦ vikingaheimar.is/en. May–Aug daily 9am–6pm. 1500kr. MAP P.85, POCKET MAP S2

Despite their reputation as fearsome warriors, the Vikings were also great traders and travellers, and the centrepiece of Vikingheimar is the *Íslendingur*,

a full-sized replica **Viking longship**. Before finding a home here, this working model crossed the Atlantic in 2000 to celebrate Leifur Eiríksson's discovery of "Vinland" (America), one thousand years earlier. The clinker-built wooden vessel is broad-beamed and must have been fairly stable, but it would still have taken some nerve to brave an Atlantic crossing without so much as a cabin to shelter under; you can walk around on deck, imagining what being crammed alongside a bunch of seasick freebooters and their livestock must have been like. Aside from the ship, the museum has an account of the brief Viking settlement of Vinland (poor rations and harsh weather eventually drove them back) and some period remains found locally, plus a multimedia exhibition on Viking myths.

Lava tubes

Underneath the Reykjanes Peninsula's grey-green tumble of volcanic rubble is a complex network of **lava tubes**, many of which are unexplored. These tunnels were created when the sides of long, narrow lava flows cooled enough to harden and form an insulating tube around the molten centre, which continued to flow until the tunnel drained. Later eruptions buried the tubes, and they'd be unknown today if cave-ins hadn't revealed their presence. More are being discovered every year, but the current pick includes kilometre-long **Raufarhólshellir**, with its weird ice formations; the similarly scaled **Búri Cave**, only found in 2005; spectacular **Þríhnúkagígur** (though this is actually a drained magma chamber, rather than a tube); and **Leiðarendi**, which is perhaps the least exciting, but also the most accessible. Because of the dangers inherent in exploring the tubes, you should only visit them as part of a tour (9,500–39,000kr/person); try ⓦextremeiceland.is or ⓦinsidethevolcano.com.

HAFNABERG CLIFFS

West off Route 425, about 5km south of Hafnir village. MAP P.85, POCKET MAP S3

Iceland's old roadways were once marked by strings of large **stone cairns** known as "priests" (because, quip locals, they showed the path to salvation without ever taking it themselves). One such row survives on Reykjanes, with its tail-end marking a footpath leading 3km west from a roadside parking bay to the **Hafnaberg Cliffs**; along the way you need to watch out for overly protective greater skuas, which nest in the soft sand hereabouts. The cliffs themselves drop sheer into the sea, packed through the summer with thousands of nesting seabirds. Take care near the crumbly edges.

BRIDGE BETWEEN TWO CONTINENTS

Beside Route 425, about 2km south from the Hafnaberg car park. Free. MAP P.85, POCKET MAP S3

The discrepancy between this structure's rather grand title and its appearance – an unimpressive metal footbridge crossing a small ravine – can't help but raise a smile. The gap that the **Bridge Between Two Continents** spans is supposedly part of the rift system where the North American and Eurasian continental plates are tearing apart. Nonetheless, it's all a bit ludicrous, and the "Welcome to America" and "Welcome to Europe" signs at either end – not to mention the monochrome gravel and black-sand scenery – add to the sense of fun.

REYKJANESTÁ

Off Route 425 along a 2km-long good gravel road signposted "Reykjanesviti". MAP P.85, POCKET MAP S3

Reykjanestá is the Reykjanes Peninsula's southwestern extremity, a rocky, storm-battered headland whose geothermal potential is being tapped by **Reykjanesvirkjun**, the shiny 100MW power station that you pass on the way in. There's another thermal outlet nearby at **Gunnuhver hot springs**, a compact mess of boiling mud, hissing vents and clouds of sulphurous steam, which last blew itself apart in 2005 – check out the skeletons of boardwalks still dangling over the void. Traces of older building foundations are evidence of former efforts to establish vegetable hothouses here.

Reykjanestá's main vehicle track ends at a coastal car park, where a tall white **lighthouse** stands slightly inland on a hillock; the original was sited on the grassy coastal headland opposite, but fell into the sea during an earthquake. A solidified lava flow from some ancient eruption forms a low platform above the waves; far out to sea you can just pick out the remote sea stack of **Eldey**, which hosts Europe's largest gannet colony. Eldey also has the sad distinction of being where the last known pair of great auks was bludgeoned to death in 1844; there's a giant **bronze auk** in the Reykjanestá car park as a memorial, its beak pointing seawards.

KVIKAN MUSEUM

Hafnargata 12a, Grindavík ⓦ grindavik.is /kvikan. Daily 10am–5pm. 1200kr. MAP P.85

There are three separate exhibitions at Kvikan, but two – one on geothermal power, and another about local author and Spanish scholar Guðberg Bergsson – can safely be skipped in favour of **Saltfisk- setur Íslands** (Icelandic Saltfish Museum). Even today, with tourism replacing fishing as Iceland's main source of income, the country owes a great deal to the cod: the national **coat of arms** was originally a golden cod, filleted and crowned on a red field, and the Icelandic Nobel Laureate, Halldor Laxnes, wasn't exaggerating when he made the memorable comment, "*Lifið er saltfiskur*" ("life is saltfish"), back in the 1930s. Even so, a lack of timber for boatbuilding meant that Iceland only really became a fishing nation during the late nineteenth century, after the first modern vessels could be imported, but its success swiftly drew farmers off the land to settle in new coastal settlements around the country. Today, saltfish still accounts for a good slice of Iceland's export earnings, with most of the product shipped to Spain and West Africa. The Saltfish Museum covers all this history brilliantly in models, dioramas, old photographs and – somehow – the authentic smell of salted cod.

SELATANGAR

12km east of Grindavík on Route 427, then south along short gravel road. MAP P.85, POCKET MAP T3

Selatangar was once an important seasonal fishing camp for southwestern Iceland, and though abandoned after better ports with modern vessels became established elsewhere during the nineteenth century, many of the settlement's **stone-block** structures survive among an eerie coastal landscape of grey sand and ancient, disinte- grating lava flows. It's reached from the car park along a 200m-long path marked out with driftwood and other bits of flotsam, but you probably won't realize that you've arrived anywhere until you begin to notice small, roofless huts and walled-up recesses – careful investigation will uncover well over a dozen – all half- camouflaged among the volcanic boulders.

Selatangar must have been a tough place to live even in summer, given the pernicious fogs which keep materializing and dispersing along with the coastal breeze. Stories of hauntings by a lonely **ghost** named Tanga-Tómas add to the decidedly spooky atmosphere.

KRÝSUVÍKURBERG

22km from Grindavík on Route 427, then turn south at a signpost marked "Krýsuvíkurbjarg" along a 4km gravel road. Be prepared to park the car and walk in if the road proves impassable. MAP P.85, POCKET MAP T3

On a sunny day, the seascapes from the top of **Krýsuvíkurberg** – a long, crescent-shaped bay of cliffs – are fabulous, the blue waters below contrasting with a clifftop layer of ochre soil and green grass. You might be lucky and see a couple of **puffins** here, but the main inhabitants at Krýsuvíkurberg are thousands of fulmars and kittiwakes, all of which you can hear long before you reach the top. The main headland is topped by a **triangulation point**, which makes a great spot to admire the scenery, from where you can follow the ridges inland and back around to the car park along unmarked tracks.

STRANDARKIRKJA

Off the eastern end of Route 427, about 15km from Þorlákshöfn, via a short sealed road. MAP P.85, POCKET MAP T3

A neat, unassuming weatherboard church painted dove grey and black, Strandarkirkja – the "**Church on the Seashore**" – was built around 1900 by grateful fishermen after they survived a shipwreck off the local coast. There was once a busy community here, but today only the church and a handful of scattered farm buildings remain; it's a beautiful spot however, with green meadows protected from the seafront by a high stone wall. Walk along the shore and you'll probably see seals and plenty of eider ducks, but watch out if you try to stroll through the arctic tern colony along the approach road – they can get a bit nasty.

Cafés and restaurants

BRYGGJAN

Miðgarði 2, Grindavík ☎ 426 7100. Daily 8am–10pm. MAP P.85

This cosy harbour restaurant is full of maritime memorabilia: sextants, ships' bells, and even the shell of a huge spider crab. They do coffee, waffles and light meals, including tasty lobster soup with home-made bread (1800kr). Outdoor tables for sunny days, too.

KAFFI DUUS

Duusgata 10, Keflavík ☎ 421 7080. ⓦ duus .is/en. Daily 11am–11pm. MAP P.85

At first glance a straightforward place, but it's not just the tandoori chicken (4200kr) which has an Asian slant:

Indian spices also seep into the bacon-wrapped monkfish (4150kr) and battered cod and chips (4100kr). Pricey, but there are sea views and generous portions.

BRYGGJAN

T-BÆR CAFÉ

LAVA RESTAURANT

Blue Lagoon ☎ 420 8800, ⓦ bluelagoon.com.
Daily: June–Aug noon–9pm; Sept–May
noon–8.30pm. MAP P.85

Set right against a lava wall
with views out over the
lagoon, this place certainly
enjoys a superb setting. The
menu features "modern
Icelandic" cuisine: their rack
of lamb is excellent, as are the
langoustine and fish of the
day. Fixed-price lunches
(5900kr) are decent value
considering the location,
though dinner is expensive.

PAPA'S

Opposite Kvikan museum at Hafnargata 7a,
Grindavík ☎ 426 9955, ⓦ papas.is. Daily
noon–10pm. MAP P.85

Grill house serving good cod
and chips (2400kr), though
their pizzas really steal the
show: a "supreme" with
everything is 2950kr, but best
is the "TNT", loaded with
pepperoni, black pepper,
chillies and jalapeno sauce
(2050kr).

PYLSUVAGN

Strandarkirkja, near the campsite. No phone.
Daily 10am–10pm. MAP P.85

This yellow mobile trailer sells
canned drinks and, more
importantly, *pylsur*: Icelandic
hot dogs served with copious
fried onions and remoulade
sauce (700kr). There's an
adjacent shelter shed with
chairs and tables if the
weather's bad.

T-BÆR CAFÉ

Between the campsite and church,
Strandarkirkja ☎ 483 3150. Mon–Wed &
Fri–Sun 10am–10pm, Thurs 2–10pm.
MAP P.85

A long, low wooden building
in the middle of nowhere
which serves great light meals,
coffee and cakes: try the lamb
stew, cheesecake or pancakes
with rhubarb jam (each
around 1700kr). Often
surprisingly busy given the
location. Not much English
spoken.

THAI KEFLAVÍK

Hafnargata 39, Keflavík ☎ 421 8666,
ⓦ thaikeflavik.is. Mon–Fri 11.30am–10pm,
Sat & Sun 4–10pm. MAP P.85

This place, with a plain white
interior and wooden tables, is
popular for its good-value
spicy soups, noodles, red
curries and deep fried fish
(nothing over 2000kr), though
the best deal is their lunchtime
buffet at 1490kr.

The Golden Circle

Spreading eastwards from Reykjavík, the route known as the Golden Circle ties together some of Iceland's most iconic landscapes and historic sights. The centrepiece is Þingvellir, a monumental rift valley where Iceland's original parliament met in Viking times, while the nearby cathedral at Skálholt once served as one of the country's two greatest religious pivots (along with Hólar in northern Iceland). Elsewhere, a web of roads weaves through the lush summertime landscape of meadows framed by distant snowcapped peaks, where you could spend a mellow half-day comparing the relative attractions of outdoor hot pools at Fontana Spa (luxurious) and the so-called "Secret Lagoon" (minimalist). Routes ultimately converge right on the edge of Iceland's barren wilds at Geysir, the original geyser after which all others are named, and the mighty waterfall of Gullfoss.

ÞINGVELLIR NATIONAL PARK

30km northeast of Reykjavík on Route 36
ⓦ thingvellir.is/english.aspx. Free. MAP P.92.
POCKET MAP U1

Þingvellir – the "Assembly Plains" – fill a 4km-wide, 40m-deep rift valley that marks where the North American and Eurasian continental plates are tearing apart at the rate of 1.5cm every year. It was in this dramatic landscape that Iceland's entire population first gathered in the tenth century to hold an annual assembly, thereby establishing a system of government which survived, in one form or another, for nearly a thousand years (see box opposite).

Orientate yourself at the viewpoint next to the Visitor Centre on Route 36. South lies Iceland's largest lake, Þingvallavatn, from where the rift valley runs northeast for 16km, covered in a tangle of dwarf birch thickets and flanked by basalt columns, to Skjaldbreiður's distant, flattened cone – at 1060m, one of the highest peaks in view.

From the viewpoint, a footpath descends into the 2km-long Almannagjá canyon past Lögberg, the rock from where Iceland's laws were publicly recited in Viking times. Look out too for traces of *buðs*, roofed camps built as accommodation during assemblies. The path continues to where the narrow Öxará – the Axe River – splashes down into the rift over the western escarpment; the rocks midstream are barely worn, supporting the story that the river was diverted during the tenth century to provide drinking water for the thirty thousand or so people who converged on Þingvellir each year. Under medieval Danish law, the site became an execution ground for witches and adulterers.

The Alþing

From 960, Iceland's 36 regional chieftains convened the Alþing, or General Assembly, at Þingvellir for two weeks every summer. Almost the entire Icelandic population attended the event: tented camps were set up, people traded, gossiped, settled disputes at the four regional courts and listened to the **Lawspeaker** reciting the country's legal code. The highest penalty was being declared an "out-law" – banishment from Iceland for three years – yet, although the courts carried great authority, they had no concrete powers to enforce their decisions beyond making them public knowledge. If litigants felt themselves strong enough to ignore the courts they could do so, though at the risk that others would seek satisfaction privately. *Njál's Saga* (see box, p.100) contains a graphic account of such a battle between two feuding clans, which broke out at the Alþing itself in 1011 AD.

It was the Alþing's lack of real power that allowed Norway and then Denmark to take control of the country during the Middle Ages; by the late thirteenth century the lawspeaker's position was abolished and the courts stripped of all legislative authority. Though Iceland's Alþing survives to this day, restored with full powers after Independence from Denmark in 1944, the **last assembly** at Þingvellir was in 1798, after which the parliament relocated to Reykjavík.

East over the river, Þingvellir's plain white **church** sits on a small rise, the only substantial building in the valley. The original structure was built in 1080 with support from the Norwegian king, though the present building dates from 1859. Two tombs out the back belong to the poets Einar Benediktsson and Jónas Hallgrímsson, both major forces in Iceland's nineteenth-century drive for political independence from Denmark; it's fitting that they were buried in a location so strongly tied to the national identity. While you're here, don't overlook Flosagjá and Peningagjá, deep volcanic fissures nearby, flooded by clear blue spring water.

ÞINGVELLIR NATIONAL PARK

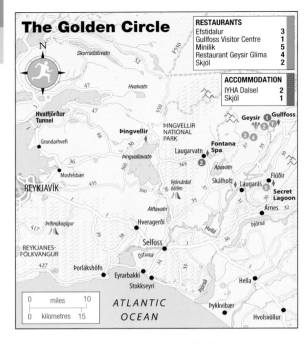

The Golden Circle

N

RESTAURANTS	
Efstidalur	3
Gullfoss Visitor Centre	1
Minilik	5
Restaurant Geysir Glíma	4
Skjól	2

ACCOMMODATION	
IYHA Dalsel	2
Skjól	1

Skorradalsvatn

Hvalvatn

Þingvellir

Hvalfjörður Tunnel

Grundarhvefi

Þingvellir NATIONAL PARK

Mosfelsbær

Þingvallavatn

REYKJAVÍK

Geysir   Gullfoss

Fontana Spa

Laugarvatn

Apavatn

Þjórsárdal 669m

Skálholt

Laugarás

Flúðir

Secret Lagoon

Árnes

Álftavatn

Hveragerði

Hvítá

Þjórsá

Prihnúkagigur

REYKJANES-FÓLKVANGUR

Selfoss

Ölfusá

Þorlákshöfn

Eyrarbakki

Hella

Stokkseyri

0	miles	10
0	kilometres	15

ATLANTIC OCEAN

Þykkvibær

Hvolsvöllur

FONTANA SPA

Hverabraut 1, Laugarvatn, 75km east of Reykjavík; turn off Route 37 at the N1 roadhouse and follow the signs ⓦ fontana.is. Mid-May to Sept 10am–11pm; Oct to mid-May 11am–9pm. 3400kr. MAP P.92, POCKET MAP V2

This small open-air spa overlooks the lakeshore at the tiny resort town of **Laugarvatn** – which, in typical Icelandic style, isn't much more than a few houses. Fontana itself sits literally on top of a cauldron of bubbling hot springs, which splutter and hiss noisily below the sauna huts, pouring out erratic clouds of steam. There are also a couple of more sedate tiled thermal pools; they're very shallow, though – better for sitting in with a beer ordered from the bar (there's also a café that serves light meals) than for swimming. Visiting after dark in winter is quite an experience,

especially when the northern lights are putting on a show.

SKÁLHOLT

Off Route 35 on Route 31, 85km east of Reykjavík. Daily 10am–5pm. Free. MAP P.92, POCKET MAP V2

The lush farming region above the middle Hvítá – one of

FONTANA SPA

Iceland's longest rivers – is known as the "Bishop's Tongue". That might be because this is church land, overlooked from the top of a knoll by the historic Skálholt cathedral, which was founded as early as 1056 AD (Christianity had only been introduced in 1000). The site went on to become a bustling centre of learning with a population in excess of two hundred people, making it the country's largest medieval settlement. The original wooden cathedral was eventually destroyed by an earthquake in the late eighteenth century, and the current black-and-white building was only built and reconsecrated in 1963.

The **interior** is fairly sober, with abstract stained-glass windows and a tapestry-like mosaic of Christ behind the altar providing the only colour; during the summer the stone sarcophagus belonging to Bishop Páll Jónsson, a charismatic thirteenth-century churchman, is also on view.

Outside, recent archeological excavations have exposed the foundations of the former bishop's residence, and there's also a monument to Iceland's last Catholic bishop, Jón Arason, who was executed here during the sixteenth-century religious wars.

SKÁLHOLT

SECRET LAGOON

Off Route 30, at Hverahólmi, Flúðir, 100km east of Reykjavík; head north out of town and turn east immediately over the bridge ☎ 555 3351, 🌐 gamlalaugin.is. May–Sept daily 10am–10pm; Oct–April Mon–Thurs & Sun 2–6pm, Fri & Sat 2–8pm. 2500kr. MAP P.92

In contrast to the higher-profile Blue Lagoon and Fontana Spa, the "Secret Lagoon" is a decidedly low-tech affair – basically a large outdoor pond full of gently steaming water. Purpose-built for recreation in the 1890s, it fell into disrepair after more modern swimming pools sprung up in neighbouring towns, and has only recently been renovated and reopened for general use.

Touring the Golden Circle

Renting a car (see p.127) is the least expensive way for more than one person to cover the Golden Circle, even after factoring in fuel costs. Otherwise, the cheapest deal is on the daily Þingvellir–Laugarvatn–Geysir–Gullfoss **bus** run by Reykjavík Excursions (8900kr return; 🌐 re.is), which stops long enough at each place to have a brief look around. For a dedicated, nine-hour **Golden Circle Tour**, there's Reykjavík Excursions again (9900kr), Gray Line (🌐 grayline.is; 9500kr) and Sterna (🌐 sterna.is; 9300kr), not to mention a host of smaller operators. It's best to book a day in advance in summer; all can collect from Reykjavík accommodation, and a guide provides commentary in English en route.

GEYSIR

Right beside Route 35, 100km east of Reykjavík. Open access. Free. MAP P.92, POCKET MAP V1

The Geysir thermal area occupies the edge of a grassy plain below Bjaranarfell's 720m-high slopes, with steam from the dozen or so geysers here visible long before you arrive. The largest vent, **Geysir** itself, has been pretty much inactive for the last few decades. Instead, join the crowds surrounding **Strokkur**, "the Churn", which reliably fires its load 30m skywards every few minutes. Nobody is sure exactly what causes the eruptions, but watch closely and you'll see a dome of cooler water form on top of Strokkur's pool just before an eruption, which some experts believe acts as a "lid", allowing the pressure below to build up to bursting point. Take time to look at some of the smaller, less active vents, especially **Blesi**'s twin pools – one clear and colourless, the other opaque blue. There are no protective barriers at Geysir, in spite of the boiling hot pools; keep children supervised and under no circumstances put any part of your body in the springs.

STROKKUR

GULLFOSS

Route 35, about 107km east of Reykjavík. Open access. Free. MAP P.92, POCKET MAP V1

Saved for the nation from being flooded by a hydro dam back in the 1920s, Gullfoss – the Golden Falls – forms a spectacular, thundering twin cataract across the Hvítá River: entering the mouth of a basalt gorge, the river drops 10m and then turns sharply, falling a further 20m into a sunless chasm from which spray fountains upwards in huge, soggy clouds, catching rainbows and giving the falls their name. Adding to the spectacle is the location: look back the way you've come and all is green, but turn north and vistas take in a stark gravel plain spreading towards the distant mountain ridges and ice caps of Iceland's barren Interior (see p.108). In winter, the canyon is covered in curtains of ice, and the falls, brought nearly to a standstill by the freeze, are eerily silent. The best viewing place is from the top of the gorge; you can also walk right up to the canyon's edge above the waterfall, but take care on the wet rocks. Note that there are no substantial safety barriers at the site.

GULLFOSS

Restaurants

EFSTIDALUR

Route 37, about 15km east from Laugarvatn and Fontana Spa towards Geysir ☎ 486 1186, ⓦ efstidalur.is. Daily 11am–10pm. MAP P.92

Smart hotel restaurant surrounded by beautiful farmland, serving easily the best food in the region, much of it locally sourced. Try smoked trout or soup (1250–1950kr), or a home-reared steak (4600kr).

GULLFOSS VISITOR CENTRE RESTAURANT

Gullfoss, right next to the car park and lookout. No phone. Daily 9am–9.30pm. MAP P.92

Timber-framed building with glass feature windows offering superlative mountain views. Try their lamb stew (1950kr); much else is ordinary and overpriced.

MINILIK

Hrunamannavegur (Route 30), Flúðir ☎ 846 9798, ⓦ minilik.is. Opening hours variable, so call ahead to check. MAP P.92

Iceland's sole Ethiopian restaurant is loudly striped in green, yellow and red. Dishes are tangy, sour and spicy and served with traditional *njeera*, (fermented dough pancakes) – try them with *awaze tibs* (a fried

EFSTIDALUR

lamb dish). Plenty of vegetarian options, and excellent coffee. Bank on around 3000kr a head.

RESTAURANT GEYSIR GLÍMA

At the Visitor Centre, Geysir. No phone. Daily 10am–5pm. MAP P.92

Despite the chic, Nordic-minimalist decor (pine ceiling, slate floor and basalt-block walls), and its obvious potential as a tourist trap, prices are pretty reasonable here: you can get quiche and salad for 1790kr or a pizza from 1550kr, with even better deals in the separate canteen around the corner. This was the site of Iceland's first wrestling school, explaining the unusual photo display.

SKJÓL

Route 35, halfway between Geysir and Gullfoss ☎ 899 4541. Daily from late morning until midnight. MAP P.92

This dark timber, lodge-style bar, stuck out in a lonely field between two of Iceland's most touristed attractions (the owner clearly knew what he was doing when he picked this location), is good for a convivial after-tour drink, some conversation and a bar snack, though they also do tasty pizza and grills for under 2000kr.

RESTAURANT GEYSIR GLIMA

The south coast

Heading east from Reykjavík, Highway 1 (the Ringroad) runs parallel to the coast for 185km through a well-watered region of rolling green pasture – home to Iceland's major horse stud farms – and down to the country's southernmost point near the pleasant seaside village of Vík. The final third of the journey passes within sight of the Eyjafjallajökull and Mýrdalsjökull ice caps; Eyjafjallajökull's 1666m apex is southwestern Iceland's highest point, and site of the volcanic eruption in 2010 which grounded aircraft across Europe. Along the way are hothouses at Hveragerði, some key saga landscapes, stunning waterfalls at Seljalandsfoss and Skógar, one of the country's best hiking trails, plus some bizarre black-sand beaches. Offshore, a ferry can whisk you over to impressive cliffs, volcanoes and puffin colonies at Heimaey, largest of the Westman Islands.

HVERAGERÐI

Ringroad, 40km southeast of Reykjavík. Tourist office inside the shopping centre at the entrance to town: Mon–Fri 9am–6pm, Sat 9am–4pm, Sun 9am–2pm ☎ 483 4601, ⊛ south.is. Geothermal Park at Hveramörk 13. Mon–Sat 9am–6pm, Sun 10am–4pm. 250kr, mud bath 750kr. MAP PP.98–99, POCKET MAP U2

HVERAGERÐI

Sitting astride a patently active geothermal area, **Hveragerði** comprises a compact grid of homes just north of the Ringroad, all overlooked by a crumpled mass of steaming hills. This was the first place in Iceland to harness underground heat for agriculture back in the 1920s, and almost half the buildings in town are **hothouses**, growing a year-round supply of fresh vegetables and exotic, colourful garden plants. Other attractions include a **crevasse** which opened up during an earthquake in 2008 and today runs right through the tourist office, and a **Geothermal Park** by the church, which sports steaming vents, bubbling mud pools and even a miniature geyser. Ask at the tourist office about half-day **hiking trails** into the hills behind town, where there are more hissing steam vents and a shallow thermal stream in which you can enjoy a warm soak.

SELFOSS

Ringroad, 57km southeast of Reykjavik;
Kerið crater is 15km north on Route 35.
MAP PP.98–99, POCKET MAP U2

The main landmark at **Selfoss**,
a large service town on the
fast-flowing Ölfusá, is its
substantial **suspension bridge**,
which first opened in 1891 and
immediately drew business
away from the small river ferry
which used to operate
downstream. Homes and shops
set up around the new crossing,
and gradually Iceland's first
inland town took shape. The
original bridge – whose
construction caused a major
strike, after labourers were only
given fresh salmon to eat –
collapsed in the 1940s, when
two milk trucks tried to cross it
at the same time. Aside from
this, the sole sight nearby is
little **Kerið** crater, a 70m-deep,
flooded volcanic depression
formed from deep red scoria
gravel. Selfoss is also something
of a gateway: the Ringroad
continues eastwards over the
well-watered plains of the lower
Þjórsá and Rangá river systems,
while north are routes to the
Golden Circle and Interior.

KERID

STOKKSEYRI AND EYRARBAKKI

Route 34, 15km south of Selfoss. Ghost
Centre at Hafnargata 9, Stokkseyri
ⓦ icelandicwonders.com. 2000kr. MAP PP.98–99,
POCKET MAP U3

Insignificant today, these two
pretty seaside villages have a
rich historical heritage – and
excellent **restaurants** (see
p.105). The former fishing
hamlet of **Stokkseyri** was once
an important port, though when
you stand on the stone storm
wall and gaze out across the
seaweed-strewn rocks and reefs,
it's hard to imagine fishermen
launching their heavy rowing
boats from such an inhospitable
shore. The old fish-processing
factory incorporates a **Ghost
Centre**, a slightly tacky take on
Icelandic folklore.

About 4km west, larger
Eyrarbakki houses a prison
and an attractive core of old
wooden homes, but is
principally famous for being
where Bjarni Herjólfsson set
sail in 985 on a voyage which
accidentally took him within
sight of North America. He
later told Leifur Eiríksson
about his discovery, and so it
was Leifur who became the
first known European to make
landfall in the Americas, or
"Vinland" as he called it after
the vines that grew there.

STOKKSEYRI

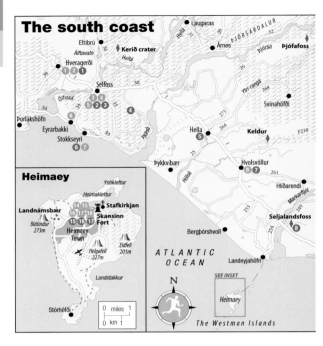

The south coast

Heimaey

KELDUR

Off the Ringroad 95km southeast of
Reykjavík, then 20km north on Route 264.
The final few kilometres are on a good
gravel road. June 15–Aug 15 daily 9am–5pm.
700kr. MAP PP.98–99, POCKET MAP V3

Though a little off the beaten
track, saga associations make
the detour to **Keldur** a
rewarding trip. This pretty farm
sits amid fields on the edge of
an overgrown lava flow, with
the cloud-smudged **Hekla
volcano** (see p.110) as a
backdrop. Most of its buildings
are recent, but the estate dates
to Viking times and parts of a
traditional turf-roofed block
here might well be over eight
hundred years old: the
structural beams are dated to
the seventeenth century, but
wall panels are decorated with
simple line engravings, typical
of the Viking period. Of similar

vintage is the rough-hewn
tunnel under the house
(sometimes open to the public),
which was built as an escape
route in case of siege. It's
believed that **Snorri
Sturlusson**, Iceland's great
medieval man of letters, was
raised at Keldur.

THE SAGA CENTRE

100km southeast of Reykjavík along the
Ringroad at Hlíðarvegur 14, Hvolsvöllur
☏ 487 8781. May 15–Sept 15 daily 9am–6pm;
Sept 15–May 15 Sat & Sun 10am–5pm. 950kr.
MAP PP.98–99

Hvolsvöllur's absorbing **Saga
Centre** needs a good hour of
your time. Most of the museum
explores the Viking period
through detailed information
boards, photos of important
sites, models, dioramas, replicas
of clothes and weapons, and
maps of the routes that these
great naval navigators and

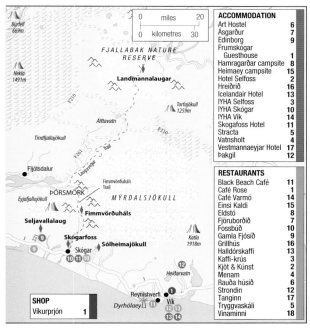

ACCOMMODATION	
Art Hostel	6
Ásgarður	7
Edinborg	9
Frumskógar Guesthouse	1
Hamragarðar campsite	8
Heimaey campsite	15
Hotel Selfoss	2
Hreiðrið	16
Icelandair Hotel	13
IYHA Selfoss	3
IYHA Skógar	10
IYHA Vík	14
Skogafoss Hotel	11
Stracta	5
Vatnsholt	4
Vestmannaeyjar Hotel	17
Þakgil	12

RESTAURANTS	
Black Beach Café	11
Café Rose	1
Café Varmó	14
Einsi Kaldi	15
Eldstó	8
Fjöruborðið	7
Fossbúð	10
Gamla Fjósíð	9
Grillhús	16
Halldórskaffi	13
Kaffi-krús	3
Kjöt & Kúnst	2
Menam	4
Rauða húsíð	6
Strondin	12
Tanginn	17
Tryggvaskáli	5
Vinaminni	18

SHOP	
Vikurprjón	1

explorers took on their wanderings. Ask too about progress on a modern project to create a 90m-long, Bayeux-like **tapestry** of *Njál's Saga* (see box, p.100), featuring all the major episodes from the tale.

SELJALANDSFOSS

120km southeast of Reykjavík at the junction of the Ringroad and Route 249.
MAP PP.98–99, POCKET MAP W3

East from Hvolsvöllur, just past the turning to Landeyjahöfn and the ferry port for Heimaey (see p.104), Route 249 branches north towards Þórsmörk (p.112). Almost immediately you reach **Seljalandsfoss**, an impressive **waterfall** that drops 60m off the long, undercut hillside into a shallow pool. There are good views from slopes off to one side, and a footpath runs right behind the curtain – expect a good

soaking from the spray. It's especially photogenic on summer evenings, when the low sun catches the spray and makes the falls glow gold. Walk along the cliff and you'll find several smaller falls too, one of which, **Gljúfrafoss**, is almost hidden inside the cliff-face.

SELJALANDSFOSS

Njál's Saga

With its hardboiled narrative, a deep streak of dark humour and deadpan descriptions of shocking violence, **Njál's Saga** paints a vivid picture of clan warfare in tenth-century Iceland. The story centres on the life of the far-sighted Njál Þorgeirsson and his great friend, the heroic and generous Gunnar Hámundarson, whose lives are pitched against the evil schemings of Mörð Valgarðsson. Jealous of Gunnar's popularity, Mörð manipulates a succession of disreputable characters into picking fights with him, and Gunnar is eventually branded a troublemaker and exiled from Iceland at the Alþing law courts (see box, p.91). When he refuses to leave, a vengeful posse led by Mörð lays siege to his home, finally killing him after his spiteful wife refuses to help defend the house – inspiring Gunnar's memorable comment, "To each their own way of earning fame".

Meanwhile, encouraged by Mörð, Njál's sons carry out their own vendettas against a rival clan. After peace talks break down, Njál and almost his entire family are driven into their house and burned to death, an event which deeply divides the country. The sole survivor, Kári, chases "the Burners" overseas, where he hunts them down, one at a time. But his anger eventually subsides, and he makes a pilgrimage to seek absolution from the pope before returning to Iceland, where all the players in the saga finally make peace.

EYJAFJALLAJÖKULL ERUPTS VISITOR CENTRE

Ringroad 140km southeast of Reykjavík. Daily: June–Aug 9am–6pm; Sept–May 11am–4pm. Toilet €1. Film 800kr. MAP PP.98–99, POCKET MAP W4

The huge rocky platform above Seljalandsfoss supports the Eyjafjallajökull ice cap, under which slumbers the **volcano** which awoke in 2010 to wreak havoc with Europe's aircraft. The Eyjafjallajökull Erupts Visitor Centre is a monument to those events, screening a twenty-minute long documentary about Þorvaldseyri farm, directly over the road, whose buildings and fields were buried under the huge fallout of volcanic ash. There's incredible footage of lava spilling out from the eruption site in the hills, and of a shock wave visibly exploding out

SELJAVALLALAUG

through the clouds, but the most moving moment is the heartbreaking sight of the farmer's face when he first returns home. Light relief is provided by a run of foreign **newsreaders** attempting to pronounce "Eyjafjallajökull".

SELJAVALLALAUG

Ringroad 140km southeast of Reykjavik, then north along gravel Route 242 for a few kilometres to a parking area. Free. MAP PP.98–99, POCKET MAP W3

Just a short drive from the Eyjafjallajökull Erupts Visitor Centre, and then a fifteen-minute walk along a rubble-filled gorge, Seljavallalaug is a fairly shallow, rectangular **swimming pool** fed by a hot spring. It was just about buried by ash from the 2010 eruption – though you can't see the ice cap itself from here, you're right under the edge of the Eyjafjallajökull plateau – but the pool is now clean again, and having an outdoor soak amid the wild scenery is a quintessentially Icelandic experience.

Fimmvörðuháls hike

The 25km-long trail from **Skógar** (see p.102) to **Þórsmörk** (see p.112), via the Fimmvörðuháls pass between the Eyjafjallajökull and Mýrdalsjökull ice caps, is one of Iceland's best – and most demanding – day hikes. It's usually accessible without equipment from mid-June to September, though you always need to come prepared for rain and snow, poor visibility and cold. The track is erratically pegged, so carry a compass and a suitable map.

From the top of Skógafoss the trail follows the river uphill past many small **waterfalls**. Some 8km along there's a footbridge and the landscape changes to a dark, rocky plain, gradually climbing to snowfields. Along the way you pass **two hiking huts** (you need to book beds via ⌨ utivist.is) and a pale blue tarn at **Fimmvörðuháls** (1043m), the flat pass in between the two glaciers. You end up at the top of a steep, 100m snowfield with dramatic views down into Þórsmörk; the quickest way down is to cautiously slide it on your backside. At the bottom is a short but scary traverse across a narrow ledge to the flat, muddy plateau of **Morinsheiði**, from where a relatively straightforward descent lands you at Þórsmörk. Allow at least eight hours for the journey, even in good weather.

SKÓGAR

Ringroad, 155km southeast of Reykjavík.
Folk Museum 🌐 skogasafn.is. Daily: June–
Aug 9am–6pm; Sept–May 11am–4pm. 2000kr.
MAP PP.98–99, POCKET MAP W4

There's very little to the hamlet of Skógar – not even a proper shop or fuel pump – and there'd be no reason to stop if it weren't for a stunning waterfall, plus an unusually interesting museum. Invisible from the road, the waterfall – **Skógarfoss** – is a 62m-high monster: stand in front of it (if the outward blast of air doesn't knock you over) and the world disappears amid roaring waters and spray. There's a metal staircase to the top and the start of the muddy moorland trail up over the mountains towards Þórsmörk (see p.112), with long views seawards to Heimaey.

Across the hamlet, Skógar's **Folk Museum** sketches out the region's history through an eclectic collection which takes in everything from nineteenth-century wooden fishing boats and turf farmhouses to a copy of the Bible dating from 1584, a Viking cloak pin, and a brass ring from a treasure chest which some stingy farmer – who didn't want his children to inherit his wealth – had thrown into the pool at Skógarfoss.

SÓLHEIMAJÖKULL

153km southeast along the Ringroad from Reykjavík, then 5km north along the gravel Route 221. MAP PP.98–99, POCKET MAP W3

Immediately over the shallow, glacier-fed Jökulsá Fulilækur, turn north off the Ringroad and follow the track to a parking area. From here it's a fifteen-minute walk to the front of Sólheimajökull, a narrow but substantial **glacier** descending off the Mýrdalsjökull ice cap. As they move under their own colossal weight, Iceland's glaciers grind the rocks below into black gravel and sand which makes the ice tongues look "dirty", but Sólheimajökull is certainly impressive, deeply streaked in crevasses. Don't approach too close, as the glacier front is unstable.

VIEW FROM DYRHÓLAEY

DYRHÓLAEY

165km southeast along the Ringroad from
Reykjavík, then 6km south on Route 218.
MAP PP.98–99, POCKET MAP W4

Dyrhólaey is Iceland's
southernmost point, a dramatic
set of basalt cliffs jutting out to
sea over a long expanse of black
sand. There's a lighthouse, and
the cliffs are pierced by a huge
arch – not visible from here,
though *Black Beach Café* (see
p.105) at Reynishverfi makes a
fine vantage point – that is
large enough for a yacht to pass
beneath. Dyrhólaey's grassy
tops are also riddled with
puffin burrows, occupied by
breeding birds throughout
the summer.

REYNISHVERFI

175km southeast of the Ringroad from
Reykjavík, then 6km south on Route 215.
MAP PP.98–99, POCKET MAP W4

East of Dyrhólaey the view is
blocked by Reynisfjall, a ridge
of hills running to the sea. At
its southwestern tip lies
Reynishverfi, an attractive
shingle beach with treacherous
waves (don't get too close) and
a steep cliff faced in twisted

basalt columns. Down the
beach is a large cave, while the
offshore stacks are the Troll
Rocks, which are better viewed
from Vík.

VÍK

Ringroad, 185km southeast of Reykjavík.
MAP PP.98–99, POCKET MAP X4

A pretty coastal village caught
between Reynisfjall's steep,
sodden slopes and a deadening
expanse of volcanic desert to
the east, Vík started life as a
trading station during the
nineteenth century and has
since expanded to fill a few
streets. The only sight in town
is **Brydebúð**, the original
wooden general store around
which Vík coalesced, which
now serves as an information
centre, local history museum,
and a restaurant. The road runs
500m past Brydebúð and down
to a parking bay above the sea,
beyond which lies Reynisfjall's
southernmost cliffs, packed
with nesting seabirds, three
tall spires offshore known as
Reynisdrangar – the **Troll
Rocks** – and a long, black-sand
beach stretching eastwards to
the horizon.

Getting to Heimaey

The Herjólfur car and passenger **ferry** to Heimaey (☎ 482 2800, ⦿ herjolfur.is) departs several times a day from **Landeyjahöfn**, 15km south off the Ringroad at Seljalandsfoss (see p.99) via Route 254. Pedestrians 1260kr each way; cars 2660kr plus 1260kr/person. For **flights from Reykjavík** contact Eagle Air (☎ 562 2640, ⦿ eagleair.is). The fare is 19,000kr each way, with online discounts available.

HEIMAEY

Natural History Museum, Heiðarvegur 12 ⦿ saeheimar.is. May–Sept daily 10am–5pm; Oct–April Sat 1–4pm. 1000kr. Eldheimar museum, Helgafellsbraut ☎ 488 2000, ⦿ eldheimar.is. Daily 11am–6pm. 2600kr including audioguide. MAP PP.98–99, POCKET MAP V4

The volcanic **Westman Islands**, 10km off Iceland's southwest coast, all formed over the last few thousand years – though the youngest, Surtsey, popped out of the waves as recently as the 1960s.

The only inhabited island in the group, Heimaey, is also the largest at 6km long, and the ferry (see box above) docks alongside fishing boats right in the middle of Heimaey town. Aim first for the **Natural History Museum**, where the highlight is a tame, orphaned puffin which you can handle. Around the harbour, Skansinn is a reconstructed thirteenth-century stone fort, while Stafkirkjan is a traditional wooden church, built in the Viking style in 2000. Inland, paths lead through the rough mass of the Kirkjubærhraun lavafield and up to the summit of Eldfell volcano, whose 1973 eruption nearly destroyed the town. For more on this event, visit the superb **Eldheimar museum**, built around the excavated remains of a house which was completely buried under ash. To see puffins in the wild you'll need to hike 6km south to Stórhöfði headland, whose grassy slopes are riddled through summer with their burrows.

STAFKIRKJAN, HEIMAEY

Shop

VÍKURPRJÓN

Next to the N1 fuel station on the Ringroad, Vík. Daily 7.30am–10.30pm. MAP PP.98–99
This factory outlet has made a name for itself with the quality of its woollens – everything from traditional heavy-duty Icelandic jumpers to hats, gloves and blankets. The ground floor has all the tourist tat; head upstairs for outdoor wear and lower prices.

Cafés and restaurants

BLACK BEACH CAFÉ

Reynishverfi ☎ 571 2718, ⓦ blackbeach.is. Daily 11am–10pm; à la carte 6–9pm. MAP PP.98–99
A modern glass-fronted affair, built of black basalt blocks and perfectly camouflaged against the cliffs, this makes a perfect spot to withdraw from bad weather and enjoy a warming bowl of lamb soup (1690kr), pan-fried char (3790kr) or just a cake and coffee (990kr). Don't miss the superb views down the coast to Dyrhólaey's arch (see p.103).

CAFÉ ROSE

At the corner of Breiðamörk and Austurmörk, Hveragerði ☎ 483 1100. Daily noon–9pm. MAP PP.98–99
Unadorned but friendly fast-food grillhouse serving crêpes, burgers and pizza from around 1500kr. They do decent coffee too, and beer on tap in the evenings.

CAFÉ VARMÓ

At the corner of Herjolfsgata and Strandvegur, Haeimay ☎ 481 1674. Mon–Fri 9am–6pm. MAP PP.98–99

The plain, dated decor won't win any prizes, but prices are reasonable and if you like heavy-duty home-made cakes, or hearty lamb and barley soup that you could stand a spoon up in, you've come to the right place.

EINSI KALDI

At the Vestmannaeyjar hotel, Vestmannabraut 28, Heimaey ☎ 481 2900. Daily 11am–2pm & 5–9pm. MAP PP.98–99
Smart and expensive restaurant inside the town's only real hotel. Safe bets are the succulent monkfish (3890kr), lamb fillet with thyme (5200kr) or the lobster tails (6190kr); if your conscience allows it, this would be the place to sample the local speciality – smoked puffin (2590kr).

ELDSTÓ

Austurvegur 2, Hvolsvöllur ☎ 482 1011, ⓦ eldsto.is. Restaurant daily 11am–10pm. MAP PP.98–99
Pottery, gallery and café inside a comfy, old-style timber-and-tin building. Variable quality, but on a good day the Greek salad (2090kr) or tasty house burgers (2490kr) do the job well. Cake and coffee is always good (990kr).

FJÖRUBORÐIÐ

Eyrarbraut 3a, Stokkseyri ☎ 483 1550, ⓦ fjorubordid.is. Daily noon–9pm. MAP PP.98–99
Lobster restaurants have flourished in Iceland over the last few years, and this is one of the best – not least for the location, inside a wooden shack up against the sea wall at no-horse Stokkseyri village (see p.97). They sell fifteen tons of lobster a year; a set meal of lobster soup, 300g of langoustine tails and a dessert costs 8400kr, but you could always just order the soup (2700kr) or 250g of tails (4700kr).

KJÖT & KÚNST

FOSSBÚÐ

On the road to the falls, Skógar ☎ 487 8843.
Daily 7am–9pm. MAP PP.98–99

The only non-hotel restaurant
in Skógar, serving basic, filling,
plain food – sandwiches,
burgers, soup, buns and
chips – at very reasonable
prices. The lunchtime special of
pork schnitzel, soup and coffee
costs a bargain 2500kr, very
welcome if you've just hiked in
from Þórsmörk (see p.112).

GAMLA FJÓSÍÐ

Ringroad about 2km west of the
Eyjafjallajökull Erupts Visitor Centre (see
p.100) ☎ 487 7788, ⓦ gamlafjosid.is. Daily
11am–9pm. MAP PP.98–99

Housed in a low-ceilinged
former cowshed, this comfortable café-restaurant dishes up a
range of tasty fare – burgers
(2000kr), Westman Islands
lobster (6920kr) or catch of the
day (3990kr) – but is perhaps
best known for its "Volcano
soup", a beef stew laden with
chillies (2290kr).

GRILLHÚS

Vestmannabraut, across from the
Vestmannaeyjar, Heimaey ☎ 482 1000. Daily
11am–10pm. MAP PP.98–99

No surprises what they serve at
this low-slung timber-clad
diner: T-bone steak (4990kr),
lobster burgers (2690kr), fish
and chips (2190kr) and pizza.
The delicious scent of barbecued
meat wafts around the street
outside while they're serving.

HALLDÓRSKAFFI

Inside Brydebúð, Vík ☎ 487 1202. Daily
11am–8pm. MAP PP.98–99

About half of this old timber
building is a dining room, but
it still can't cope with the
crowds who come for their
superb pizzas: a 12" seafood
special with shrimps, mussels
and tuna costs 2800kr. They
don't take bookings, so turn up
prepared to wait.

KAFFI-KRÚS

Austurvegur, Selfoss ☎ 482 1266. Daily
10am–midnight. MAP PP.98–99

One of the longest-running
cafés outside the capital, this
cosy, low-ceilinged place is best
for fine coffee, cakes and light
meals (eaten on the terrace in
good weather), though they
also do some pricey mains –
burgers, salmon or grills – at
upwards of 2500kr.

KJÖT & KÚNST

Breiðamörk 21, Hveragerði ☎ 483 5010.
Mon–Sat noon–8.30pm. MAP PP.98–99

Pouring out clouds of steam on cold days, it's hard to miss the thermal ovens outside this place, which they put to good use in preparing fish and meat dishes (4190kr), not to mention their famous *hverabrauð* (steam-baked rye bread). Not bad either for salads, grills, soup and meatballs (around 2500kr), or just a coffee.

MENAM

Eyravegur 8, Selfoss ☎ 482 4099. Daily 11.30am–2pm & 5–10pm. MAP PP.98–99

The heat and spices are toned down a bit for local tastes, but *Menam*'s traditional Thai dishes, such as green chicken curry, are packed with flavour and come with a healthy portion of rice. Excellent value, with most mains under 2600kr.

RAUÐA HÚSIÐ

Búðarstíg 4, Eyrarbakki (see p.97) ☎ 483 3330, ⓦ raudahusid.is. Mon–Thurs 11.30am–9pm, Fri–Sun 11.30am–10pm. MAP PP.98–99

Alternative to Stokkseyri's *Fjöruborðið*, though there's a wider choice of dishes besides lobster (which is also cheaper here, at 6650kr): fish of the day (4500kr), lamb fillet (5500kr) or a sampler of smoked and cured salmon (2150kr). Don't miss their warm chocolate cake for dessert. Booking essential.

STRONDIN

Austurvegur 18, Vík ☎ 487 1230. Daily 6–10pm. MAP PP.98–99

Facing seawards from behind the N1 roadhouse, *Strondin* has an outdoor terrace and glassed-in dining room for wet days. Though the decor is plain, the menu is varied: dishes cover everything from lamb stew (2100kr) to chicken pasta with basil and tomatoes (2350kr). You could also take a chance on a traditional taster of *hákarl* (fermented shark) with the essential *brennevin* chaser (2200kr).

TANGINN

Tangagata, Heimaey ☎ 414 4420, ⓦ tanginn .is. Mon–Fri 11am–11pm, Sat & Sun 11am–1am. MAP PP.98–99

Down at the harbour, this dark room with feature windows and heavy pine furniture makes a surprisingly chic setting for feasting on some excellent seafood. The mussels are a good starter (1750kr), best followed by monkfish (3290kr) or cod and chips (3190kr) – though they also serve a not-very-traditional horse fillet. Sea views make it a good place to linger over a beer on a rainy day.

TRYGGVASKÁLI

Austurvegur 1, on the roundabout by the bridge, Selfoss ☎ 482 1390 ⓦ tryggvaskali .is. Daily 11.30am–11pm. MAP PP.98–99

Hidden off the roundabout by the bridge, the oldest wooden building in Selfoss makes a smart, if quirky, setting to enjoy some excellent food – cod and kale (3950kr), lobster salad (3100kr) or slow-cooked salmon and barley (4350kr). The building has served several purposes over the years, including a hotel, and the variously sized rooms are still furnished with period fittings.

VINAMINNI

Barustígur, Heimaey ☎ 481 2424. Daily 10am–10pm. MAP PP.98–99

Not the best place on the island to eat, but long opening hours make this a convenient place to head for a coffee, and the food menu isn't bad: salmon and scrambled egg sandwiches (1250kr), pitta stuffed with various fillings (1900kr) and the inevitable pizzas and burgers (from 1700kr).

The Interior

You'd need to set aside a good week for a comprehensive trip across the heart of Iceland's Interior, a stark landscape of monochrome gravel plains, enormous ice caps and atrocious storms – but you can reach its fringes with an overnight visit. There are Viking remains at Þjórsádalur, a valley ravaged by the twelfth-century eruption of one of Iceland's most active volcanoes, Hekla; an extraordinary hot-spring bathing experience in the wilds at Landmannalaugar; and stunning highland scenery at Þórsmörk, whose horizons are hemmed in by glacier caps. With a little more time, it's also possible to walk between Landmannalaugar and Þórsmörk along one of the country's finest hiking trails – as long as you come equipped for the weather and a few relatively shallow river crossings.

STÖNG

115km east from Ryekjavík via Selfoss (see p.97) and Route 32, then 7km north along Route 327, a gravel track that can sometimes be impassable for conventional vehicles. MAP P.109, POCKET MAP W2

Iceland's longest river – the Þjórsá – exits the Interior through **Þjórsárdalur**, a once fertile valley which in 1104 was smothered under a thick blanket of volcanic ash during an eruption of Hekla, only a few kilometres to the east. Up on the valley's eastern side, ongoing excavations since the 1930s have uncovered the well-preserved remains of **Stöng**, the farmstead of Viking chieftain Gaukur Trándilsson. Protected inside a tin-roofed shed, stone foundations and postholes mark the outline of a longhouse, with the central fire pit, various halls, outhouses, animal pens and private quarters clearly visible. Not on

PJODVELDISBÆRINN

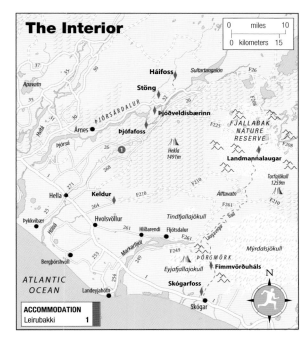

The Interior

| 0 | miles | 10 |
| 0 | kilometers | 15 |

ACCOMMODATION

Leirubakki   **1**

view are an adjoining smithy and church, which were discovered only recently.

HÁIFOSS

A 20km return hike from the car park at Stöng, or a 12km drive each way along gravel routes 327 and 332, which might be too rough for conventional vehicles. MAP P.109, POCKET MAP W2

Northeast up the valley from Stöng, Háifoss – Iceland's fourth-highest waterfall – plunges 120m off the Interior plateau in a single narrow

Seasonal access

M ost Interior roads are **four-wheel-drive only**, and even then are open for just a few months each summer, when they're covered by buses and private tours. Check sight accounts for details.

curtain, the deep, narrow canyon below undercut by the force of the water. A second falls upstream is joined to the first by a short but narrow gully.

ÞJÓÐVELDISBÆRINN

115km east from Ryekjavík via Selfoss (see p.97) and Route 32, then 500m south along a signposted track ⊕ thjodveldisbaer.is. June–Aug daily 10am–6pm. 600kr., POCKET MAP W2

To appreciate how the longhouse at Stöng originally appeared, visit nearby Þjóðveldisbærinn, a reconstructed period homestead built from hand-cut timber and roofed in thick slabs of insulating turf. Inside it's surprisingly cosy (though don't forget that livestock were penned here too, at least through the winter), and the bright furnishings suggest a comfortable – if very public – living space.

HEKLA

HEKLA

Contact Arctic Adventures (W adventures.is) for guided hikes to the summit. MAP P.109, POCKET MAP W2

With its 1500m-high summit usually hidden by cloud, Hekla – one of Iceland's most active volcanoes – is named after an expression meaning "Hooded". The mountain's regular eruptions (including the one that buried Stöng in 1104), disturbing subterranean grumblings and a belief that its sulphurous crater formed the very entrance to hell, left it unclimbed until the eighteenth century; it last stirred in February 2000, when hundreds of sightseers from Reykjavík became trapped on Hekla's foothills by a snowstorm. On clear days, its hunchbacked crest dusted in snow makes an unmistakable landmark, visible from as far away as Selfoss.

ÞJÓFAFOSS

123km east from Reykjavík via the Ringroad and Route 26, then 4km west on a good gravel track. MAP P.109, POCKET MAP V2

One of the best views to be had of Hekla is from Þjófafoss, a broad, lively waterfall just to

the west, which sits below a looming flat-topped hill in a bend of the Þjórsá. You're not only close to Hekla here, but also surrounded by a strangely attractive monochrome landscape of degraded lava and pale yellow pumice pebbles. Despite the apparent desolation and the bumpy gravel road in, this isn't a particularly difficult place to reach, providing an easy taster of the Interior's barren charms.

LANDMANNALAUGAR

175km east from Reykjavík via the Ringroad, Route 26 and the F225. Route F225 is open June–September and is four-wheel-drive only, involving soft sand and several dangerous river crossings. For summer bus schedules contact Trex (W trex.is). Jeep day-tours are run by Landmannalaugar Tours (W landmannalaugar tours.com) and Arctic Adventures (W adventures.is). POCKET MAP W2

Set amid a rugged landscape of shattered obsidian and rhyolite peaks, brightly streaked in orange, grey and green, **Landmannalaugar** is a flat-bottomed gravel valley bordered on one side by a massive fifteenth-century lava flow. Out from underneath the lava emerge two streams, one icy cold and the other scalding hot; there's a perfect wild bathing spot where the waters mix. Known for its summer pasture, Landmannalaugar was once a staging post on cross-Iceland roads, and there are some fine day-hikes in the vicinity – in good weather, don't miss the chance to ascend **Bláhnúkur** (945m), the bald peak to the south, for spectacular views. There's a clearly marked path up the north face to the top, but for a bit of excitement, try a slip-slide descent via the loose scree slopes to the west. For many, however, Landmannalaugar's appeal is in its location at the trailhead for the long-distance Laugavegur hiking route to Þórsmörk and the coast at Skógar.

LANDMANNALAUGAR

Laugavegur hike

The superb **Laugavegur hiking trail** stretches 55km between Landmannalaugar and Þórsmörk, divided into stages by huts and campsites which are grouped at regular intervals. From Þórsmörk, you can continue south over the mountains to Skógar via the Fimmvörðuhals pass (see box, p.101).

The first stage (12km) passes a steaming thermal area at Stórihver – a bizarre sight amid the snow – before ending high in the hills at **Hrafntinnusker**, a weather-beaten slope covered in obsidian boulders. From here it's another 12km over a snowy rhyolite plateau and down a steep slope to **Álftavatn**, a small lake set amid vivid green hillocks; the next stage is slightly longer and crosses a gravel desert and a couple of very shallow (but icy cold) rivers to a tiny sheltered valley at **Bótnar-Emstrur**. There are fabulous views of Entujökull, the nearest of Mýrdalsjökull's glaciers, from clifftops around 3km southeast of the hut here. The final 15km leg to **Þórsmörk** (see p.112) is over relatively dull moorland before you ford the Þröngá – the deepest river you have to ford on the trail – and enter the suddenly lush birch and juniper woodland at Þórsmörk's northern boundary, just a short walk from the huts and bus stop.

The trail is open from June until mid-September, when buses run daily from Reykjavík to the end points at Landmannalaugar and Þórsmörk (see ⓦ trex.is for bus schedules). Hikers need to carry their own food and be fully equipped for the weather conditions. For information contact the Icelandic Touring Association (ⓦ fi.is).

ÞÓRSMÖRK

ÞÓRSMÖRK

155km southeast from Reykjavík via Route 1
and the F249. The F249 is four-wheel-drive
only, involving rough gravel and dangerous
river crossings, and is only open June–
September. For bus schedules contact Trex
(W trex.is). Jeep tours run by South Iceland
Adventures (W siadv.is). MAP P.109

A beautiful highland valley,
Þórsmörk has hiking trails
running in all directions, and
thick stands of dwarf willow,
birch and wildflowers watered
by a web of glacial rivers that
flow west off the Mýrdalsjökull
ice cap. The valley is split into
three areas, each with its own
hiking hut accommodation;
isolated on the far western side
is Húsadalur (W volcanohuts.
com), Þórsmörk's main bus
terminus but still a thirty-
minute hike from the main
valley. This is split in two by
the 7km-long Krossá River, a
braided glacial flow which
originates in the ice caps that
hem everything in; to the north
of the river is Þórsmörk proper,
with a base of sorts at
Skagfjörðsskáli hut (W fi.is),
while to the south is Goðaland
and Básar hut (W utivist.is). Be
sure to cross the Krossá via the

bridge; the river is dangerously
cold and fast, and people have
drowned trying to wade over.
The best views on the river's
north side are from the top of
knuckle-like Valahnúkur, a
brief hike up on a well-
marked path; south of the
Krossá lies a more challenging
climb in the shape of
805m-high Útigönguhöfði –
the final section is incredibly
steep, with chains to help you.

WILDFLOWERS, ÞÓRSMÖRK

Þórsmörk hikes

Þórsmörk is covered in a network of excellent hiking trails, though these are not well marked on the ground and even "easy" routes tend to involve steep gradients, loose scree and occasionally high, narrow traverses. Rangers at the accommodation huts can provide useful maps, weather forecasts and general advice, though – hardened as they are to local conditions – they often underestimate potential difficulties.

The main walk from the **Skagfjörðsskáli** hut starts at the next bay east at Slyppugil, a wooded gully which you follow uphill to the jagged east–west ridge of Tindfjöll. The trail weaves along Tindfjöll's gravelly, landslip-prone north face to the solitary spire of Tröllakirkja, before emerging onto open heath at Tindfjöll's eastern end: the double-tipped cone 2km northeast is Rjúpnafell, which can be climbed up a steep, zigzag path to its 824m summit – give yourself at least five hours for the return hike from the hut.

The best excursion from the **Básar** hut is to follow the popular trail south towards Skógar (p.102) as far as the flat, muddy Morinsheiði Plateau. From here you turn west and descend to a low saddle below 805m-high Útigönguhöfði, then take a hideously steep path straight up it to the rounded peak. Views from the top are breathtaking, and there's a chain to help your descent off the far side. A low, 5km-long ridge continues west to the heights directly above Básar, with an easy descent along a path to your starting point. Again, allow five hours for the hike.

ACCOMMODATION

Accommodation

Although Reykjavík's accommodation options continue to mushroom as the tourist influx increases, pressure on beds in the summer months is always great and it's a good idea to book in advance, especially in June, July and August. Hotels do not come cheap in Reykjavík, usually hovering around 25–35,000kr for an average double room in high season. The quality is, however, generally high, though rooms can be block-like and characterless – sometimes it's the view or the location that makes it. Online discounts and opting for a shared bathroom (where available) can reduce prices significantly. Guesthouses cost around 15–20,000kr; often family run, they tend to have more character than hotels, with rooms ranging from the barely furnished to the very comfortable, and facilities are usually shared. Prices overall tend to rise by around a third during the high season (May to September); those given here are for the cheapest double room during the summer months.

At hostels, you'll find that meals are sometimes offered, though most have kitchens for self-catering. Campsites vary in size but will always have washing facilities, and sometimes a kitchen, too. Self-catering is worth considering since it will save a lot of money on eating out – one of the main expenses in Iceland.

Austurvöllur and around

BORG > Pósthússtræti 11 🕾 551 1440, 🖤 hotelborg.is. MAP PP.32–33, POCKET MAP D4. The city's very first hotel, opened in the 1930s and the unofficial home of visiting heads of state ever since. A showcase of sophistication and four-star elegance, each room is individually decorated in Art Deco style with period furniture – and prices to match. It's hard to beat the location, too, right in the heart of the Austurvöllur area, with Austurstræti and Hafnarstræti right on the doorstep. **45,000kr**

ICELANDAIR REYKJAVÍK MARINA > Mýrargata 2 🕾 444 4000, 🖤 icelandairhotels.com. MAP P.45, POCKET MAP B1. Bold, bright and refreshingly quirky, this harbourside hotel not only enjoys terrific views of the trawlers in dry dock right outside, but its rooms also have a maritime feel with a twist of chic. If you're on a stopover deal with Icelandair (see box, p.126), or are simply booking accommodation via the airline and are able to choose between this hotel and the *Icelandair Natura* (see p.120), make this one your preference. **34,500kr**

Booking ahead

In order to get the lowest room rate book well in advance via the hotel's own website or try one of the many online booking sites. If you do arrive at the last minute without a reservation, the city tourist office may be able to help at their office on Aðalstræti (see p.133). Alternatively, think about staying in Hafnarfjörður (see p.80), where pressure on beds is less intense.

PLAZA ▸ Aðalstræti 4 ☎ 595 8550, ⓦ plaza.is. MAP PP.32–33, POCKET MAP C3. The style in this tastefully renovated old building, a stone's throw from Austurstræti, is Nordic minimalism meets old-fashioned charm, with heavy wooden floors, plain white walls and immaculately tiled bathrooms complementing the high-beamed ceilings. The rooms at the front of the hotel look out over Ingolfstorg which can be noisy so it may be wise to seek out a room further back. **28,700kr**

RADISSON BLU 1919 ▸ Pósthússtræti 2 ☎ 599 1000, ⓦ radissonblu.com /1919hotel-reykjavik. MAP PP.32–33, POCKET MAP D3. Housed in the elegant former headquarters of the Eimskip shipping line, this Art Deco hotel combines old-fashioned charm with modern chic. Book one month in advance to secure the rate we have given. The penthouse suites (77,400kr) with elevated sleeping sections and separate dining area are the best Reykjavík has to offer and would make an ideal treat for a special occasion. **39,000kr**

REYKJAVÍK CENTRUM ▸ Aðalstræti 16 ☎ 514 6000, ⓦ hotelcentrum.is. MAP PP.32–33, POCKET MAP C4. Built in traditional early-1900s style, this hotel offers a curious yet pleasing mix of stylish and homely, featuring old-fashioned wallpapers and fittings. Perfectly located on Aðalstræti, it's near the action of Laugavegur as well as being ideally situated for a gentle evening stroll around Tjörnin, which is right on the doorstep. Breakfast is an extra 2200kr. **31,800kr**

REYKJAVÍK DOWNTOWN HOSTEL ▸ Vesturgata 17 ☎ 553 8120, ⓦ hostel .is. MAP P.45, POCKET MAP B2. Vesturgata is a terrific spot – it's not only perfectly located for the harbour but is also an easy saunter to the bars, shops

and restaurants around Austurstræti and Hafnarstræti. Swish and stylish, this HI place is actually more hotel than hostel, with six-berth dorms decorated in subtle pastel colours at unbeatable prices. **Dorm beds from 6150kr, double room 22,700kr**

SALVATION ARMY GUESTHOUSE ▸ Kirkjustræti 2 ☎ 561 3203, ⓦ guesthouse.is. MAP PP.32–33, POCKET MAP C4. If money's tight it's worth considering this place, the cheapest guesthouse in Reykjavík, which has been in business for years. However, it's often fully booked so it pays to reserve well in advance. Rooms here all share facilities – they may well be narrow, have clanking pipes and paper-thin walls, but the price is hard to beat and it's dead central. June–Aug only. **Dorms 15,000kr, sleeping bags 4000kr**

Tjörnin and around

HOLT ▸ Bergstaðastræti 37 ☎ 552 5700, ⓦ holt.is. MAP P.51, POCKET MAP E6. First opened in 1965, this is one of the most elegant and luxurious hotels in Reykjavík. With over three hundred paintings by Icelandic artists adorning the rooms and public areas, it's a little like staying overnight in an art gallery. Rooms are of the Persian-carpet, dark-wood-panelling, red-leather-armchair and chocolate-on-the-pillow variety. **30,000kr**

RADISSON BLU SAGA REYKJAVÍK ▸ Hagatorg ☎ 525 9900, ⓦ radissonblu .com/sagahotel-reykjavik. MAP P.51, POCKET MAP M2. This large, swanky business hotel is usually packed with conference delegates dashing up to admire the view from the top-floor restaurant. The rooms are cosmopolitan in feel and design, and feature bureaux and comfortable armchairs. Book early for the best rates. Bear in mind that it's a good thirty-minute walk from here to the shops and restaurants on Laugavegur. **27,800kr**

TRAVEL-INN > Sóleyjargata 31 ☎ 561 3553, Ⓦ dalfoss.is. MAP P.51, POCKET MAP N3. Occupying a tastefully renovated old house with good-sized, comfortable rooms overlooking the southern end of Tjörnin (and handy for the BSÍ bus station on Vatnsmýrarvegur), this is one of Reykjavik's top guesthouses. It's been in business for years and is well regarded, not least since the rooms with shared bath are exceptionally good value. Higher prices apply for stays Thurs–Sun. **15,100kr**

Laugavegur and around

BALDURSBRÁ > Laufásvegur 41 ☎ 552 6646, Ⓦ baldursbra.com. MAP P.51, POCKET MAP D7. Another of Reykjavik's long-standing accommodation options, this friendly, modern guesthouse enjoys a fantastic location, right in the city centre and overlooking Tjörnin. Though the price is good, rooms are a little cramped and the floral decor may not be to everyone's taste. The secluded garden with a hot tub for guests' use is, however, a definite boon and it's hard to find such a central location at this price. **16,900kr**

FRÓN > Laugarvegur 22A ☎ 511 4666, Ⓦ hotelfron.is. MAP PP.58–59, POCKET MAP F5. If you're self-catering, this hotel right in the city centre should be your first choice. In addition to regular double rooms, it offers stylish, modern studios (25,500kr) and larger apartments (28,800kr), each with bath, kitchenette and TV. Not only that, but the Bónus supermarket, offering the best prices on food and vegetables in town, is just across the road – perfect for when it comes to buying supplies. **24,000kr**

GUESTHOUSE 101 > Laugavegur 101 ☎ 562 6101, Ⓦ iceland101.com. MAP PP.58–59, POCKET MAP K6. What makes this guesthouse worth considering is its location – it's roughly a fifteen-minute walk along Laugavegur into the centre

and on to Lækjartorg; or there's the Hlemmur bus interchange right outside the door for longer journeys or tired legs. Prices are also reasonable, but otherwise it's a rather soulless place with cheap furniture and cell-like rooms. **14,700kr**

KLÖPP > Klapparstígur 26 ☎ 595 8520, Ⓦ centerhotels.is. MAP PP.58–59, POCKET MAP F4. Despite its bizarre name, this is one of central Reykjavik's better hotels and a sound choice: modern throughout, with all rooms boasting tasteful wooden floors, oak furniture and wall panelling. Rooms can be a little on the small side, though, so it probably pays to ask to look at more than one if you're not happy with your allocation. The breakfast room is also a little cramped. **25,000kr**

REYKJAVÍK LOFT HOSTEL > Bankastræti 7 ☎ 553 8140, Ⓦ hostel .is. MAP PP.58–59, POCKET MAP E4. The latest addition to the youth hostel scene in Reykjavik enjoys an unparalleled location right in the thick of things. There are six- to eight-bed dorms as well as private rooms. All rooms have private facilities and there's a top-floor café with balcony offering great views over the city centre. What's more, it's affilitated to HI, so there are discounts for members. **Dorms 8250kr, doubles 26,500kr**

ROOM WITH A VIEW > Laugavegur 18 ☎ 552 7262, Ⓦ roomwithaview .is. MAP PP.58–59, POCKET MAP F5. Quite simply, this place has got it right, offering a great selection of studios and apartments, all located on the sixth floor, overlooking the main shopping street, with incredible panoramic views from the shared balcony. Ten percent discount for stays of seven nights or more. **Budget studio 25,500kr, apartments 29,400kr**

SKJALDBREIÐ > Laugavegur 16 ☎ 595 8510, Ⓦ centerhotels.is. MAP PP.58–59, POCKET MAP F5. This hotel is another of Reykjavik's long-standing hotel options and it's hard to beat on several counts. True, the plain rooms sporting classic Nordic decor may be rather uninspiring, but the price for such a central location is extremely competitive:

bars, restaurants and shops are all right outside your window. Note, too, that the windows have extra sound-proofing – especially needed on raucous Friday and Saturday nights on Laugavegur. **25,000kr**

Hallgrímskirkja and around

ADAM > Skólavörðustígur 42 ☎ 896 0242, ⓦ adamhotel.com. MAP PP.66–67, POCKET MAP F6. Although this place likes to think it's a hotel, it's actually an upmarket guesthouse; the smart rooms all boast a kitchenette though some share facilities. The location is also one of its best features, with Hallgrímskirkja as its next-door neighbour. **19,100kr (Mon–Thurs with shared facilities; prices rise by about 7000kr Fri & Sat)**

CABIN > Borgartún 32 ☎ 511 6030, ⓦ hotelcabin.is. MAP P.75, POCKET MAP P2. The best rooms in this good-value place are at the front, offering great views out over the sea and Mount Esja. Warm autumn colours throughout, with lots of browns and greys making the decor pleasant and restful. The cheaper double rooms are only ten square metres in size and can feel a little cramped. Though it's a good twenty- to thirty-minute walk into the centre, there is a bus stop right outside the hotel. **20,600kr**

FOSSHÓTEL BARÓN > Barónsstígur 2–4 ☎ 562 3204, ⓦ fosshotel.is. MAP PP.66–67, POCKET MAP J5. Another good choice if you're thinking of doing a bit of self-catering, as there are microwaves in most of the en-suite doubles and studios. Throughout, the decor is neutral and modern, if unsensational, and many rooms have sea views. The thirty-plus apartments vary greatly in size, so look before you choose. Discounts for stays of three nights and over. **Doubles 25,300kr, studios 30,400kr**

FOSSHÓTEL LIND > Rauðarárstígur 18 ☎ 562 3350, ⓦ fosshotel.is. MAP PP.66–67, POCKET MAP K7. Bright, modern and functional hotel offering discounts for stays of three nights or more, and worth considering if other more central places are fully booked. Rooms are plainly decorated and unadventurous, but the location's within easy reach of Hlemmur's buses which bring the city centre to within a brief bus ride, instead of a twenty- to thirty-minute walk. **24,500kr**

FOSSHÓTEL REYKJAVÍK > Þórunnartún 1 ☎ 531 9000, ⓦ fosshotel.is. MAP PP.66–67, POCKET MAP P2. Sprawling over sixteen floors, the *Fosshótel* chain's jewel in the crown opened for business in the summer of 2015 and is Iceland's biggest hotel, boasting 320 rooms, all with magnificent views over the city and the waterfront. Rooms are sleek and elegant, there's a spa and a gym, and even a pub with a great choice of beers. Be under no illusion, though – none of this comes cheap. **36,700kr**

HLEMMUR SQUARE > Laugavegur 105 ☎ 415 1600, ⓦ hlemmursquare .com. MAP PP.66–67, POCKET MAP K6. Upmarket dorm accommodation (dorms sleep from four to fourteen) is available on the upper floors of this stylish 1930s building located right beside Hlemmur. Facilities are shared, but linen and duvets are top-notch; no sleeping bags are allowed. There are also two kitchens on site for guest use. The top floor is given over to eighteen spacious and tastefully appointed double rooms. **Dorms from 4,500kr, hotel room 35,000kr**

LEIFUR EIRÍKSSON > Skólavörðustígur 45 ☎ 562 0800, ⓦ hotelleifur.is. MAP PP.66–67, POCKET MAP G7. It's hard to imagine a hotel with such a perfect location – step outside the door and you're right in front of the Hallgrímskirkja, with all Reykjavík has to offer a short stroll down Skólavörðustígur. It's a small, friendly and neatly furnished place to boot; the top-floor rooms, built into the sloping roof, are particularly worthwhile for their excellent views. **27,000kr**

LUNA > Spítalastígur 1 (Check in at Baldursgata 36) ☎ 511 2800, ⓦ luna .is. MAP PP.66–67, POCKET MAP F6. If you're looking for spacious, beautifully decorated and superbly appointed apartments, this is the place to come.

With modern and bright studios sleeping two people and larger apartments, also for two people, with high-quality fittings, this is a real home from home. There's also a three-room penthouse for rent. **Studios 25,000kr, apartments 35,900kr**

ÓÐINSVÉ > Þórsgata 1 ☎ 511 6200, ⓦ hotelodinsve.is. MAP PP.66–67, POCKET MAP F6 Long-established place that's stylish, relaxed and within an easy trot of virtually everything – Skólavörðustígur and Laugavegur, for example, are barely five minutes' walk away. The elegantly decorated rooms have wooden floors, neutral decor, comfortable Scandinavian-style furniture, and feature work by renowned Icelandic photographer, RAX. Unfortunately, recent renovation work has pushed prices upwards and you're likely to be paying over the odds for what you're getting. **37,700kr**

Öskjuhlíð and around

BEST WESTERN REYKJAVÍK > Rauðarárstígur 37 ☎ 514 7000, ⓦ hotelreykjavik.is. MAP P.71, POCKET MAP N3. Though featuring widely on online booking sites – which can throw up some exceptionally good deals – this is a rather functional and uninspiring hotel, roughly twenty minutes' walk from the centre. The plain and simple rooms are clean and presentable, though you might find some disturbingly orange furnishings in them. Book in advance for the best rate quoted here. **32,000kr**

ICELANDAIR REYKJAVÍK NATURA > Nauthólsvegur 52 ☎ 444 4000, ⓦ icelandairhotels.com. MAP P.71, POCKET MAP N3. A busy and impersonal hotel stuffed with stopover travellers (see box, p.126). The 200-odd rooms here are nice enough, with wooden floors and comfortable modern furnishings throughout, though are on the small side. For some people, the location will be too far from the centre – it really is a bit of a trek into the centre, under subways and over bridges (30–40min), and in the evenings and at weekends buses here are rather infrequent. Free access to the hotel spa. **28,240kr**

SNORRI > Snorrabraut 61 ☎ 552 0598, ⓦ guesthousereykjavik.com. MAP P.71, POCKET MAP N3. This pebble-dashed modern block is not one of Reykjavík's most alluring, and the rooms are rather uninspiring, too. But the location is a winner, just a short walk (10–15min) from the centre, and there's a choice of shared facilities or en-suite. The hotel is also on many of the city's bus routes, which means you will be able to get around quite easily should you base yourself here. **17,600kr**

Laugardalur and around

ARCTIC COMFORT > Síðumúli 19 ☎ 588 5588, ⓦ arcticcomforthotel .is. MAP P.75, POCKET MAP Q3. Oddly located in a business district a good walk (30–40min) from the centre, it's worth considering this place only when everything else is full. Its out-of-town location is not great, but it is perfectly smart and clean and does offer good value for money. Some rooms have self-catering facilities. There are several bus routes, too, which pass close by. **22,500kr**

GRAND REYKJAVÍK > Sigtún 38 ☎ 514 8000, ⓦ grand.is. MAP P.75, POCKET MAP P2. The clue's in the name: there's no shortage of opulence here, with marble floors, stylish chrome fittings and wood panels aplenty, though for the money you may wish to be closer to the centre – it's a 25-minute walk from here. Accommodation is in two buildings – the original and a newer, shimmering high-rise tower whose rooms enjoy stunning views. **35,100kr**

HILTON REYKJAVÍK NORDICA > Suðurlandsbraut 2 ☎ 444 5000, ⓦ reykjavik.nordica.hilton.com. MAP P.75, POCKET MAP P3. The *Hilton* chain's one and only hotel in Iceland is big on Nordic minimalism: glass, chrome and natural wood are everywhere you look. Rooms at the front of the sprawling building enjoy views over the sea to Mount Esja. The hotel is popular with tour groups so it can feel rather anonymous given the number of guests here at any one time. **26,040kr**

ÍSLAND > Ármúli 9 ☎ 595 7000, Ⓦ hotelisland.is. MAP P.75, POCKET MAP Q3. Though it tends to change hands fairly frequently due to its out-of-town location, this is another of Reykjavík's long-standing and dependable accommodation options. Although a little too far from the centre to be your first choice (about 2.5km), the light and airy Scandinavian-designed rooms, with lots of wood panels, glass and chrome, make this worth considering if others are full. **29,300kr**

KRÍUNES > Við Vatnsendur ☎ 567 2245, Ⓦ kriunes.is. MAP P.75. With your own transport, it's worth considering this great little guesthouse located a fifteen-minute drive southeast of the city. A former farmhouse painted in warm Mediterranean colours and sporting lovely terracotta tiles and wooden floors, it certainly lives up to its name: sited beside the "end of the water", it enjoys a truly fantastic lakeside location, surrounded by high trees and with views of the water. **23,300kr**

REYKJAVÍK CAMPSITE > Sundlaugar vegur 32 ☎ 568 6944, Ⓦ reykjavik campsite.is. MAP P.75, POCKET MAP Q2. This is the cheapest place to stay in Reykjavík, with cooking and shower facilities on site, plus some rather small two-berth cabins with bunk beds; facilities are shared. The site is perfectly located for Iceland's biggest and best swimming pool, Laugardalslaug. The city centre, though, is a good walk away (30–40min) so it might be worth considering taking the bus if you want to save your legs. **Camping 1700kr, cabins 12,500kr**

Hafnarfjörður

CAMPSITE > Hjallabraut 51 ☎ 565 0900, Ⓦ lavahostel.is. MAP P.81. Located within leafy Víðistaðatún park, off Flókagata north of the centre, the town's quiet campsite can make a nice alternative to the much bigger and busier site in Reykjavík. It's located in a quiet spot, has access to showers, and hot

and cold running water, though for other facilities campers must use *Lava Hostel* next door. Mid-May to mid-Sept. **1250kr**

HELGUHÚS > Lækjarkinn 8 ☎ 555 2842, Ⓦ helguhus.is. MAP P.81. Named after the owner, Helga, this is one of the town's oldest accommodation options. It's a friendly, family-run guesthouse, and you'll be made to feel straight at home. There's just a handful of rather small and plainly decorated rooms which all share facilities, though there is access to a well-stocked kitchen should you choose to go self-catering. There's a larger apartment sleeping six available, too. **15,000kr**

HÓTEL VIKING > Strandgata 55 ☎ 565 1213, Ⓦ fjorukrain.is. MAP P.81. If you're looking to get your Valhalla fix, this is the place to come. The 41 en-suite rooms bristle with over-the-top Viking decor, featuring lots of heavy wooden flourishes and gothic prints hanging on the walls. Next door to the main hotel there are also fourteen new six-bed cabins. Guests have use of a sauna and hot tub. **Double rooms 22,700kr, cabins 30,600kr**

LAVA HOSTEL > Hjallabraut 51 ☎ 565 0900, Ⓦ lavahostel.is. MAP P.81. This new hostel is one of Hafnarfjörður's best-value options and makes a sound choice if you're looking for somewhere cheaper than Reykjavík. It's housed in a handsome modern timber structure next to the campsite and offers compact dorms (sleeping 4–8) as well as regular double rooms. Both dorms and rooms share facilities and look out over the park. **Dorms from 5400kr, double rooms 13,400kr**

Reykjanes

NORTHERN LIGHT INN > 1 Northern Lights Road, off the Blue Lagoon approach road ☎ 420 8900, Ⓦ nli.is. MAP P.85. This long building is half-hidden amid moss-covered lava flows, just minutes from the Blue Lagoon. Rooms are plain but comfortable, there's a cosy lounge area with large fireplace, plus great views from the restaurant. **35,900kr**

STRANDARKIRKJA CAMPSITE > Strandarkirkja road, off Route 427. No phone. MAP P.85. Spacious, grassy site close to the sea at this no-horse hamlet, run by a farmer who has installed showers, toilets, washing-up sinks and picnic tables. **Free**

Golden Circle

IYHA DALSEL > Dalbraut 10, Laugarvatn, on Route 37 near the N1 roadhouse ☎ 899 5409, ⊛ hostel.is. MAP P.92. This newly refurbished hostel is conveniently located within a short walk of Fontana Spa, roughly halfway between the main Golden Circle sights of Þingvellir to the west, and Geysir and Gullfoss to the east. **Dorms 6300kr, doubles 17,100kr**

SKJÓL > On Route 35, halfway between Geysir and Gullfoss ☎ 899 4541, ⊛ skjolcamping.com. MAP P.92. Perfectly pitched between two of the country's most famous sights, there's a large campsite here, plus nine simple hostel-style rooms (all with shared facilities) with a separate restaurant/bar on hand. **Camping per person 1200kr, hostel beds 5000kr**

South Coast

ART HOSTEL > Hafnargata 9, Stokkseyri, above the old fish factory ☎ 854 4510, ⊛ arthostel.is. MAP PP.98–99. A much cosier, more comfortable place than you'd guess from the storm-battered exterior, with a range of well-furnished dorms and doubles – some with en-suites and kitchenettes. Good sea views. **20,000kr**

ÁSGARÐUR > Hvolstrod, Hvolsvöllur, off the Ringroad up Route 261, beside the church ☎ 487 1440, ⊛ asgardurinn .is. MAP PP.98–99. Tucked into a thin belt of woodland, there's a handful of comfortable cabins here which sleep up to four, each complete with self-contained bathroom and kitchen. Camping facilities also available. **13,200kr**

EDINBORG > Lambafell, Route 242 on the Seljavallalaug road ☎ 487 1212, ⊛ greatsouth.is. MAP PP.98–99.

This tin-sided building contains a range of comfortable en-suite twins and family rooms; the clean lines and timber furnishings are smart but it's the surrounding wild scenery that is the real attraction. **25,000kr**

FRUMSKÓGAR GUESTHOUSE > Frumskógar 3, Hveragerði ☎ 896 2780, ⊛ frumskogar.is. MAP PP.98–99. Friendly, family-run guesthouse featuring small rooms with shared bathrooms and self-contained studio apartments, both with use of hot tubs and sauna. **21,500kr**

HAMRAGARÐAR CAMPSITE > Seljalandsfoss, 500m up Route 249 from the falls ☎ 866 7532 or ☎ 867 3535. MAP PP.98–99. Enjoying a wonderful setting with acres of thick grass for pitches, this site is just a short walk from the falls. There's also an indoor communal kitchen/dining room, plus a tiny bar, showers, toilets and laundry. **1300kr**

HOTEL SELFOSS > Eyravegi 2, Selfoss, close to the bridge ☎ 480 2500, ⊛ hotelselfoss.is. MAP PP.98–99. If you're after a "proper" multi-storey hotel with smart rooms and conference facilities, look no further than this dark block at the entrance to town. A good alternative to similar options in Reykjavík. **42,200kr**

ICELANDAIR HOTEL > Route 1, Vík ☎ 487 1480, ⊛ icelandairhotels .com. MAP PP.98–99. This upmarket concrete-and-glass affair sports neatly furnished en-suite doubles with pine flooring and superb feature windows, some with sea views. **32,000kr**

IYHA SELFOSS > Austurvegur 28 (the Ringroad), Selfoss ☎ 482 1600, ⊛ hostel.is. MAP PP.98–99. Occupying a renovated old house close to the bus stop, this well-equipped hostel has slightly spartan dorms, a kitchen, small hot tub and handy café. **Dorms 6300kr**

IYHA SKÓGAR > Skógar, on the falls road ☎ 487 8801, ⊛ hostel.is. MAP PP.98–99. The bunk-bed dorms and doubles are pretty ordinary but good facilities include under-floor heating, a massive stainless-steel kitchen and a communal TV and dining area. **Dorms 4100kr, doubles 10,600kr**

IYHA VÍK > Suðurvíkurvegur 5, Vík, up near the church ☏ 487 1106, ⓦ hostel .is. MAP PP.98–99. This friendly, well-equipped hostel is very popular (in spite of its slightly stuffy dorms) and boasts a modern kitchen, plus a dining room with sea views. Dorms 5400kr

SKOGAFOSS HOTEL > Skógar, on the falls road ☏ 487 8780. MAP PP.98–99. New place inside a long, single-storey building whose seventeen en-suite rooms are tidy and spacious, if a bit bland. Big breakfasts are available too, and you're just a short walk from the falls. 22,900kr

STRACTA > Rangárflatir 4, Hella, on the coastal side of Route 1 ☏ 851 8010, ⓦ stractahotel.is. MAP PP.98–99. This large, modern, disorienting complex has corridors heading off in all directions. The rooms and apartments sport wooden floors, smart bathrooms and lots of white, with a clutch of on-site hot tubs and saunas. 25,500kr

VATNSHOLT > Follow signposts 15km southeast of Selfoss via Route 305 ☏ 482 4829, ⓦ hotelvatnsholt. is. MAP PP.98–99. Located on a farm, this large guesthouse offers a choice of accommodation spread between several buildings, with and without en-suite facilities. There's a plethora of pets too, including an arctic fox and a raven. 21,000kr

ÞAKGIL > Turn inland 5km east of Vík at Höfðabrekka and follow the slow, twisting gravel Route 214 for 17km ☏ 893 4889, ⓦ thakgil.is. MAP PP.98–99. Small, isolated valley with campsite and self-contained cabins with bunks sleeping up to four. There's also a communal dining area inside a large cave, and local hiking trails. June–Aug only. 1300kr

Heimaey

HEIMAEY CAMPSITE > 1km west of town at Herjólfsdalur ☏ 846 9111. MAP PP.98–99. This site enjoys a spectacular location inside the collapsed bowl of an extinct volcano, with the grassy pitches half-encircled by high cliffs. 1300kr

HREIÐRID > Corner of Faxastígur and Heiðarvegur ☏ 481 1045, ⓦ tourist .eyjar.is. MAP PP.98–99. The owner of this budget guesthouse has lived on Heimaey for decades and knows all the island's secret spots. Rooms are on the small side and facilities are shared. 11,500kr

VESTMANNAEYJAR HOTEL > Vestmannabraut 28 ☏ 481 2900, ⓦ hotelvestmannaeyjar.is. MAP PP.98–99. A modern, welcoming venue whose spacious rooms feature polished wooden floors and leather lounges, with a hot tub for guests. 21,900kr

The Interior

HIKING HUTS > Landmannalaugar, Laugarvegur and Þórsmörk ⓦ fi.is and ⓦ utivist.is. These huts are like giant communal chalets with large kitchens, toilets, showers and basic sleeping arrangements in bunks or on mattresses on the floor. Bring sleeping bags and food. Per person 7000kr

LEIRUBAKKI > Route 26 ☏ 487 8700, ⓦ leirubakki.is. MAP P.109. This hotel and restaurant has Hekla's snow-smudged summit for a backdrop. Don't miss the outdoor lava-block "Viking Pool", which is tepid but affords great views of the mountain. Dorms 6100kr, doubles 23,400kr

ESSENTIALS

Arrival

You're most likely to arrive in Iceland at Keflavík International Airport, within a short bus ride of the capital, but there are a couple of other possibilities, depending on where you're coming from.

By air

Keflavík International Airport

(KEF; S2; ⓦkefairport.is), Iceland's major arrivals hub, is 40km west of the capital via the multi-lane Route 41 expressway. It's a small, uncomplicated affair and you'll most likely be through passport control and in the arrivals hall within half an hour or so of landing; note that the duty-free shop is by far the cheapest place to buy spirits in Iceland. There are a number of ATMs in the arrivals lobby.

Taxis to the city wait outside the airport but it's a good idea to book ahead via ⓦairporttaxi.is; the journey to Reykjavík takes around 45 minutes and costs 14,000kr for a four-passenger vehicle during normal working hours – ask around the arrivals area to find people to share the fare.

Airport buses are far cheaper than taxis, meet flights and run direct to Reykjavík (45min). Reykjavík Excursions (ⓦre.is) and Gray Line (ⓦgrayline.is) sell tickets in the arrivals terminal and charge around 2000kr to their respective downtown terminuses, or 2500kr to your accommodation. Keflanding (ⓦkeflanding.com) is the cheapest option at 1600kr, but you need to book online and they run fewer services. For around 8500kr, you can also arrange airport–city transfers via the Blue Lagoon – a great introduction to Iceland, or a good final stop before leaving the country.

Reyjavík City Airport (RVK; ⓦisavia.is) is right on Reykjavík's southern outskirts and handles international flights from the Faroe Islands and Greenland, as well as domestic services from around the country. Catch Strætó bus #15 (400kr; 5min) or a taxi (1500kr; 5min) into the city.

By ferry

The **Norröna International Ferry** (ⓦsmyrilline.com) runs a Denmark–Faroes–Iceland route. This is worth considering if you want to bring your own vehicle to Iceland, though you land right across the country at Seyðisfjörður, 675km from Reykjavík. One-way fares from Denmark are €427 per person for one vehicle and two people sleeping in a couchette; a private cabin costs €574 per person. If you arrive by ferry but without your own vehicle, first catch a local bus to Egilsstaðir (45min; 1050kr) and then fly to Reykjavík (ⓦairiceland.is; online fare 8000kr).

Getting around

Reykjavík's centre is so small that you can walk right across it in 30min, though city buses, bicycles and taxis come in handy for reaching some of the outlying sights and districts. For trips beyond the Greater Reykjavík area you'll need to make use of long-distance buses, car rental or tours – and, just possibly, a flight.

Stopovers

Icelandair (ⓦicelandair.com) will allow a stopover in Iceland for up to seven nights at no extra cost to your transatlantic ticket.

City bus

Strætó (ⓦstraeto.is) operate a network of numbered city buses, with the main terminus just east of the city centre at **Hlemmur Square**. Services run Mon–Fri 6.35am–midnight, Sat 7.30am–midnight and Sun 9.30am–midnight; English-language timetables can be downloaded from their website. Tickets cost 400kr a ride (pay on the bus, exact change only), with books of nine tickets (3500kr) available on buses, or good-value one-day (1000kr) or three-day (2500kr) passes from newsagents around Hlemmur Square.

Taxi

Cabs are relatively inexpensive, and 1500–2000kr should get you across town; tipping is not expected. The main ranks are on Lækjargata; between Bankstræti and Amtmannsstígur; outside the Harpa concert hall; and in the vicinity of Hallgrímskirkja. For bookings, try Hreyfill (ⓣ588 5522, ⓦhreyfill.is) or BSR (ⓣ561 0000, ⓦbsr.is).

Bicycle

Reykjavík is comfortably scaled for riding a **bicycle** around, and you can also explore most of southern Iceland with a solid mountain bike or robust tourer. If you haven't brought your own along with you, bikes can be **rented** from some accommodation or from Reykjavik Bike Tours (ⓦicelandbike.com), who also run a range of guided trips – expect to pay around 5000kr per day for a town bike, or 7250kr for something more sturdy. You should wear a helmet and weatherproof gear and, especially if you're venturing along some of the rougher roads outside the city, carry plenty of spares and a good-quality toolkit. In the countryside it's also wise to bring more than enough food and water, as it can be a very long way between shops and settlements. If it all gets too much, put your bike **on a bus** for 3500kr.

Long-distance bus

Long-distance buses cover much of the country, but not all year round. The most comprehensive coverage is provided by **Strætó** (ⓦstraeto.is), whose long-distance terminus is at Mjódd, 4km southeast of the city centre (catch bus #11 from the city terminus at Hlemmur); they run west to various locations on Reykjanes, as well as east along the Ringroad to Vík. Ringroad destinations are also covered by **Reykjavík Experience** (ⓦre.is), based at the BSÍ bus station, 500m south of the centre of town at Vatnsmýrarvegi 10, who also run a bus to Geysir and Gullfoss; and **Sterna** (ⓦsternatravel.com), whose main desk is at the Harpa Concert Hall (see p.46). For Interior destinations, **Trex** (ⓦtrex.is) operate daily from Reykjavík to Þórsmörk and Landmannalaugar, but only through the summer – roughly mid-June to early September.

Tickets for all these can be bought on the day, but it's best to book a couple of days in advance.

Weather and road conditions

Keep up to speed with English-language **weather forecasts** at ⓦen.vedur.is, which gives appraisals for the week ahead. If you're travelling around outside of Reykjavík, check up-to-the-minute **road conditions** at ⓦroad.is, with online access to cameras and colour-coded maps.

Car

For a short trip to Iceland, a **car** gives you the flexibility you need for exploring outside the capital and will get you to many places not covered by buses. **Rental costs** are fairly competitive, especially if booked in advance or if you're visiting outside the June–September peak tourist season, when rates are lower. Companies either fix a daily maximum distance (say 100km) for the rental period, or allow unlimited mileage; **optional insurance** against windscreen damage, gravel damage, and how much of the **CDW** (Collision Damage Waiver) you'll be liable for, can double the daily rental cost. A general-purpose **two- or four-door**, capable of handling all the main roads and the better gravel tracks, will cost around 9000kr per day; a **camper van** will be at least 25,000kr a day (though you'll save on accommodation costs), while a **four-wheel-drive** – only advised if you have previous experience and want to reach Landmannalaugar or Þórsmörk under your own steam – costs upwards of 20,000kr. **Fuel** costs around 225kr per litre.

Vehicles are left-hand drives and you drive on the right. The speed limit is 50km/h in built-up areas, 90km/h on surfaced roads, and 80km/h on gravel. Seat belts are compulsory for all passengers, and headlights must be on at least half-beam all the time. **Road signs** include "Einbreið brú", indicating a single-lane bridge, and "Malbik endar", marking the end of a surfaced road. General warning signs are orange and marked "Varuð" or "Hætta" (warning or hazard).

Potential problems include having other vehicles spray you with windscreen-cracking gravel – so, when passing another car, slow down and pull over as far as possible, especially on unsurfaced roads. Outside the city, beware of the possibility of livestock wandering about. On gravel, or in snow and ice (very unlikely during the summer), avoid skidding by keeping your speed down and applying the brakes slowly and as little as possible. In winter, rental vehicles are fitted with studded snow tyres, but you should carry food, water and a good blanket or sleeping bag in case your car gets stuck.

Flights

With the exception of the flight to Heimaey (see p.104), it's unlikely that you'll make use of Iceland's domestic airlines, Air Iceland (ⓦairiceland.is) and Eagle Air (ⓦeagleair.is), at least for transport. But both also offer air tours over famous landscapes such as Hekla, Eyjafjallajökull, Þingvellir and Þórsmörk, lasting around 1hr 30min (€390) – check their websites for details.

Safe travel

If you're planning to hike, cycle or drive into Iceland's remoter corners, sign up first with ⓦsafetravel.is. The website provides alerts for hiking trail and highland road conditions, plus advice on how to prepare for your trip, and allows you to leave a travel plan and contact information with them, which will be followed up if you fail to report back at the appointed time.

In case of an emergency, **call 112**. For those with smartphones, there's also a free **112 app** available, which, when activated, transmits your location and nominated contact information to the rescue services.

Activities

Tours

Tours range from whale-watching cruises (see box, p.47) to hikes, pony treks (see p.130), cycle explorations of the city (see p.127), bus safaris and sightseeing flights (see p.128). Some, like the popular Golden Circle tour that takes in Þingvellir, Geysir and Gullfoss, you can do independently without too much bother, but in other cases you'll find that organized tours are the only practical way to reach an offbeat destination.

The widest range is offered between June and September. In the October–May low season, the roads to Landmannalaugar and Þórsmörk will be impassable and operators concentrate on Northern Lights, four-wheel- driving and glacier exploration along the fringes of the southern ice caps. **Booking in advance** is always advisable, whatever the time of year.

Swimming

Swimming is a major social activity in Iceland and almost every settlement has an outdoor swimming pool, geothermally heated to 28°C, along with hot pots (hot tubs) at 35–40°C, and a sauna or steam room. Out in the wilds, hot pots are replaced by natural hot springs, such as those at Landmannalaugar. Other than Laugardalslaug (see p.75), one of the most central pools in the city itself is the popular **Sundhöllin** at Baróns-stígur 45A (☎411 5350, ⊛itr .is; Mon–Thurs 6.30am–10pm, Fri 6.30am–8pm, Sat 8am–4pm, Sun 10am–6pm; 650kr; map p66–67, Pocket map H7), where there's a 25m indoor pool, two outdoor hot pots, plus single-sex nude sunbathing terraces. The construction of a new outdoor pool here is under way.

When using an Icelandic swimming pool, take off your shoes before entering the changing rooms and leave them in the rack provided; leave your towel in the shower area between the changing rooms and the pool, not in your locker (so you can dry off before returning to the changing rooms); and shower fully, with soap and without swimwear, before getting into the pool. Though there are always separate male and female changing rooms, very few pools have private cubicles.

Hiking

Southern Iceland is crossed by a web of **hiking trails**, the best known of which is the five-day Laugarvegur track between Landmannalaugar and Skógar via Þórsmörk (see box, p.111). But there are also plenty of much shorter hikes, lasting just a few hours, such as in the hills behind Hveragerði (see p.96) and various spots along the Reykjanes coast. Be aware, though, that even popular routes are seldom well marked; you'll always need to be competent at using navigational aids, especially in poor weather. It's also prudent to seek local advice about routes, though many make light of difficulties: a "straightforward" trail might involve traversing knife-edge ridges or dangerously loose scree slopes.

Always carry warm, weatherproof **clothing**, and wear tough hiking boots; being prepared means you can still get out and enjoy yourself in bad weather. You'll also need food and water, a torch, lighter, penknife, first-aid kit, a foil insulation blanket and a whistle or mirror for attracting attention; be sure to memorize Iceland's **emergency numbers** (see box, p.130). The prime hiking months are June through to August, when the weather is relatively warm, flowers are in bloom, and the wildlife is out and about – though even then you might experience snow inland.

Iceland has two main **hiking organizations**: Ferðafélag Íslands (Touring Club of Iceland; Mörkin 6, IS-108 Reykjavík, ☎568 2533, ⓦfi.is); and Útivist (Hallaveigarstigur 1, IS-101 Reykjavík, ☎561 4330, ⓦutivist.is). Contact them for general hiking information, group treks and to **book huts** at Landmannalaugar and Þórsmörk, and along Laugavegur.

Horseriding

Horses came to Iceland with the first Viking settlers, and have remained true to their original stocky Scandinavian breed. They're sturdy, even-tempered creatures and, in addition to the usual walk, trot, gallop and canter, can move smoothly across rough ground using the gliding *tölt* gait. Horses are available for hire from farms right across southern Iceland, but to organize something in advance, check out Íshestar (ⓦishestar.is) or Eldhestar (ⓦeldhestar.is), which run treks lasting between an hour and several days for all experience levels.

Snow and action sports

There's not a huge enthusiasm for **skiing and snowboarding** in Iceland, perhaps because snow has generally been seen as just something you have to put up with. The main centre is around 20km from Reykjavík at **Bláfjöll** (ⓦskidasvaedi. is), where there are a few short slopes and a ski lift, though this is only open through the winter months.

Surprisingly, one of the world's greatest freshwater **scuba dives** is at Silfra near Þingvellir, featuring ice-blue water with truly stunning visibility. You need to be already certified and, ideally, have dry-suit skills; contact Dive Iceland (ⓦdive.is) or Dive Silfra (ⓦdivesilfra.is) for further details.

Directory A–Z

Addresses

Addresses in Iceland are given with the street name followed by the house number, post code and place i.e. "Hverfisgata 29, 101 Reykjavík".

Cinema

The multiplex Háskólabíó cinema (Hagatorg, ☎591 5145, ⓦbio.is; map p.51, Pocket map M3), attached to the university, is Reykjavík's main picture house. It screens mainstream film productions and is the only cinema in the country with Dolby Digital 3D.

Crime

Reykjavík is a relatively safe place with low levels of crime, most of it opportunistic: don't walk around the downtown area alone late at night, or leave valuables lying about or on show in a parked car, and you'll have few problems. The police (*lögreglan*) are English-speaking, unarmed and keen to help, should you need them; for general information dial ☎569 9020 or, in an **emergency**, ☎112.

Electricity

Electricity is 240v, 50Hz AC. Plugs and sockets are two-pin round prongs; make sure you carry an adaptor.

Embassies & consulates

Canada Túngata 14, 101 Reykjavík ☎575 6500, ⓦcanadainternational .gc.ca; **China** Bríetartún 1, 105 Reykjavík ☎527 6688, ⓦchina -embassy.is; **Denmark** Hverfisgata 29, 101 Reykjavík ☎575 0300,

Emergency numbers

In an emergency, dial ☎112 for fire, ambulance or police.

@island.um.dk; **Finland** Túngata 30, 101 Reykjavík @510 0100, @finland .is; **France** Tungata 22, 101 Reykjavík @575 9601, @ambafrance.is; **Germany** Laufásvegur 31, 101 Reykjavík @530 1100, @Reykjavík .diplo.de; **Greenland** Hverfisgata 29, 101 Reykjavík @575 0300, @island .um.dk; **Norway** Fjólugata 17, 101 Reykjavík @520 0700, @noregur.is; **Sweden** Lágmúli 7 @520 1230, @swedenabroad.com; **UK** Laufásvegur 31, 101 Reykjavík @550 5100 @britishembassy.is; **USA** Laufásvegur 21, 101 Reykjavík @595 2200, @iceland.usembassy.gov.

Gay and lesbian travellers

Given that Iceland is a fairly liberal country – former prime minister Jóhanna Sigurðardóttir was the world's first openly lesbian head of government – there's little discrimination and, consequently, no specifically gay venues in Reykjavík. For listings check out @gayice.is, or for general information contact the Icelandic gay and lesbian association, Samtökin 78 (Laugavegur 3, Reykjavík @552 7878, @samtokin78.is).

Health

Reykjavík's health services are modern and efficient, and all doctors will speak English. No vaccinations are required for visitors to Iceland. Water is safe to drink everywhere.

In an **emergency**, dial @112 or get to Landspítali Emergency Department, Fossvogur, 108 Reykjavík (open 24hr; Pocket map p.N3). For less urgent treatment, Reykjavík has fifteen medical centres (*heilsugaeslan*); your accommodation can contactone for you, or there's a list available at @heilsugaeslan .is/stadsetning. For free treatment, Scandinavian citizens must show medical insurance and a valid

passport, while citizens of the European Economic Area need their European Health Insurance Card and passport. Otherwise you'll need to pay at the time and then claim back the money from travel insurance.

For **emergency dental treatment** only, contact Tannlaeknavaktin at Skipholt 33 (daily 8am–10pm; @426 8000, @tannlaeknavaktin.is), around a twenty-minute walk east of Hallgrímskirkja.

There are no 24hr **pharmacies** (*apotek*) in Reykjavík, but one of the longest-opening is Lyfja at Lágmúli 5, 108 Reykjavík (daily 8am–1am; @533 2300). It's around 2km east of Hallgrímskirkja.

Internet

Iceland is one of the highest per-capita users of the internet. Most Reykjavík cafés and accommodation provide free wi-fi for customers, and getting connected is seldom a problem in the city.

Left luggage

If your accommodation can't store luggage for you, there are lockers at the BSÍ bus station, Vatnsmýrarvegi 10 (open 24hr; maximum three days); the Reykjavík City Airport terminal (open 30min before first flight in the morning and closes 30min after last arrival in the evening; maximum thirty days); and at Keflavík International Airport (daily 5am–5pm; maximum thirty days).

Money

Icelandic krónur (Isk, Ikr or kr) come in 5000kr, 2000kr, 1000kr and 500kr notes, with 100kr, 50kr, 10kr, 5kr and 1kr coins. There are plenty of banks with ATMs in central Reykjavík and larger towns; you can also find ATMs at some country fuel stations. However, you can pay for almost anything in Iceland using bank debit or credit cards (Visa and Mastercard are the most widely accepted), and it's quite feasible to spend a week here without using cash – except on Strætó buses (see p.127).

Opening hours

Generally, business hours are Monday to Friday 10am–6pm and Saturday 10am until mid-afternoon; if they open on Sunday, it will probably be after noon. In Reykjavík and larger towns, supermarkets open daily from 10am until late afternoon; in smaller communities, however, some places don't open at all at weekends. Country fuel stations provide some services for travellers, and larger ones tend to open daily 9am–10pm. Office hours are Monday to Friday 9am–5pm.

Phones

Icelandic phone numbers are seven digits long, with no area codes. Phone directories are ordered by Christian name – Jakob Gunnarsson, for example, would be listed under J, not G. Landline rates are cheapest for domestic calls at weekends and 7pm–8am Monday–Friday; on calls to Europe daily 7pm–8am; and to everywhere else daily 11pm–8am.

Iceland uses both GSM and NMT (Nordic Mobile Telephone) mobile phone networks. GSM covers Reykjavík and almost all the surrounding region; coming from the UK or EU, your own country's pay-as-you-go SIM cards might work with varying roaming rates, or buy a new pay-as-you-go SIM from fuel stations or newsagents in Iceland. You'll only need NMT coverage for remoter interior regions; contact Icelandic car rental companies or hiking organizations (see p.130) for more information.

Post

Post offices are open Monday to Friday 9am–4.30pm, though a few in Reykjavík have longer hours. Domestic mail takes around two working days; count on three to five days for mail to reach the UK or US, and a week to ten days to reach Australia and New Zealand. Anything up to 50g costs 153kr within Iceland, 180kr to Europe, and 240kr to anywhere else; up to 100g costs 185/310/490kr. For parcel rates, check Ⓦ postur.is.

Safety

You need to be responsible for your own safety in Iceland; there are so many natural hazards that it is impossible to fence them all off, and you shouldn't expect to find warning signs, safety barriers or guide ropes even at extremely dangerous locations, such as the edge of waterfalls, volcanoes or boiling mud pits.

The summer sun is strong, especially when reflected off ice or snow, so use sunscreen and sunglasses. Moisturizer and lip balm help protect against cold dry air, wind and dust.

Hypothermia – when your core body temperature drops dangerously – occurs if you get simultaneously exhausted, wet and cold; symptoms include a weak pulse, disorientation, numbness and slurred speech. Treatment involves getting as dry and as warm as possible, and taking sugary drinks – though not alcohol. Serious cases need hospital treat-ment. Avoid hypothermia by eating sufficient carbohydrates, drinking plenty of water and wearing warm and weatherproof clothing.

Smoking

Smoking is banned indoors in public buildings, restaurants, bars and cafés, and on school grounds, sport facilities or public areas of apartment buildings. Smoking is also prohibited inside most accommodation. You need to be at least 18 years old to purchase cigarettes, which are only sold by convenience stores and a few bars.

Tax refunds
If you spend more than 4000kr in any single transaction on goods to take out of the country, you are entitled to a tax refund of fifteen percent of the total price, as long as you leave Iceland within ninety days. Ask for a **Refund Tax Free form** when you make your purchases, which needs to be filled out by the shop. Money can be refunded in full back onto your credit/debit card at refund points located in the departure halls at Keflavík and Reykjavík airports; on board all international cruise ships two hours before departure; or at Reykjavík port's Visitor Centre. The same places, plus refund points at Kringlan Shopping Mall and Reykjavík's Tourist Information centres (see p.133), can make the refund in cash, but this incurs a commission.

Time
Iceland is on Greenwich Mean Time (GMT) year-round. GMT is five hours ahead of US Eastern Standard Time and ten hours behind Australian Eastern Standard Time.

Tipping
Tipping is not expected anywhere in Iceland, including for service in hotels, restaurants and taxis.

Tourist information
The **Reykjavík Tourist Office** is in the heart of the old town at Aðalstræti 2 (June until mid-Sept daily 8.30am–7pm; mid-Sept until May Mon–Fri 9am–6pm, Sat 9am–4pm, Sun 9am–2pm; ☎590 1550, ⓦ visitreykjavik.is). They're a useful source of information for local events, and can also help organize or advise about tours, accommodation and car rental. It's also worth checking out **Reykjavík Grapevine** (ⓦ grapevine.is), an irreverent weekly listings magazine which reviews attractions, parties, bands, restaurants and forthcoming events.

Travellers with disabilities
Icelandic hotels are required by law to make a percentage of their rooms accessible. Transport – including ferries, airlines and some tour buses – can make provisions for wheelchair users if notified in advance.

Reykjavík's Disabled Association, Sjálfsbjörg, is at Hátún 12, 105 Reykjavík (☎550 0360, ⓦ sjalfsbjorg .is, ⓔ sjalfsbjorg@sjalfsbjorg.is), and can advise on accessible accommodation and travel around Iceland.

Travelling with children
Reykjavík's supermarkets and pharmacies are well stocked with nappies and formula (though keep in mind where the next shops might be in the countryside). If the weather is bad, swimming pools – some of which have waterslides – make great places for children to let off steam.

Be aware that special care needs to be taken at outdoor sites (see opposite).

Festivals & events

Though Iceland's calendar is essentially Christian, many official holidays and festivals have a secular theme.

ÞORRABLÓT

February

A midwinter feast once honouring the Viking weather god Þorri. People eat traditional foods such as *svið* (sheep's head) and *hákarl* (fermented shark).

BJÓRDAGUR (BEER DAY)

March 1

Festival honouring the date in 1989 that Iceland's 74-year-old prohibition on beer was lifted. Best experienced by joining in a *rúntur* (bar crawl).

SJOMANNADAGUR (SEAMEN'S DAY)

June 4

Expect mock sea-rescue demonstrations, swimming races and tug-of-war battles, especially around Reykjavík's old harbour.

INDEPENDENCE DAY

June 17

The day the Icelandic state separated from Denmark in 1944. Low-key events held in central Reykjavík.

JÓNSMESSA

June 24

Magical creatures are said to be out in force, playing tricks on the unwary. Some people celebrate with a big bonfire; others roll around naked in the morning dew.

VERSLUNNARMANNAHELGI (LABOUR DAY WEEKEND)

First weekend in August

Traditionally, everybody heads into the countryside, sets up camp, and parties themselves into oblivion.

ÞJÓDHÁTÍÐ

First weekend in August

Held inside an extinct volcano crater on Heimaey (see p.104), and celebrated in much the same spirit as Labour Day on the mainland. Book transport and accommodation a year in advance.

RETTIR

Autumn

The *rettir*, or stock round-up, takes place in rural areas throughout September. Horses and sheep are herded from the higher summer pastures to be penned; some farms allow visitors to watch or even participate.

Public holiday dates

Jan 1 New Year's Day
March/April Maundy Thursday, Good Friday, Easter Sunday, Easter Monday
April, first Thursday after April 18 First day of summer
May 1 May Day
May/June Ascension Day, Whit Sunday, Whit Monday
June 17 National Day
August Bank Holiday (first Monday)
Dec 24–26 Christmas Eve, Christmas Day, Boxing Day
Dec 31 New Year's Eve

Chronology

16 million years ago > As the Eurasian and North American tectonic plates begin to tear apart, Iceland first pops out of the waves during volcanic eruptions.

300 BC > Historian Pytheas of Marseille writes about a frozen Arctic land named "Ultima Thule", possibly Iceland.

c.800 AD > Christian monks from Ireland settle the southern coast.

c.850 > A Viking adventurer named Naddoddur accidentally discovers Iceland.

874 > Norwegian-born Ingólfur Arnarson settles the area of Reykjavík ("Smoky Bay"), becoming the country's first known resident.

870–930 > Vikings, mostly from Norway, colonize all Iceland during the Landnám, or Settlement Period.

930 > Iceland declares itself a Commonwealth, with an annual parliament held at Þingvellir.

980–1000 > Vikings discover Greenland and North America.

1000 > Christianity becomes Iceland's national religion.

1104 > Hekla erupts violently, burying farms across the south of the country.

1220–62 > The "Sturlung Age" ushers in a period of civil war; many of Iceland's historic sagas are written down, extolling the virtues of earlier times.

1262 > The "Old Treaty" cedes Icelandic sovereignty to Norway, ending the civil war.

1280 > The *Jónsbók* of laws is compiled.

1397 > The Kalmar Union sees Norway, and hence Iceland, brought under Danish rule.

1402 > Plague arrives in Iceland and kills almost half the population.

1420–1532 > Denmark, England and Germany tussle over Icelandic trading rights during the "English Century".

1550 > As the Reformation sweeps Europe, Iceland's last Catholic bishop, Jón Arason, is executed at Skálholt and the country becomes Lutheran.

1602 > Denmark imposes a repressive trade monopoly on Iceland, beggaring the country and reducing the population to the status of tenant farmers.

1752 > Bailif Skúli Magnússon founds an Icelandic trading company, whose warehouses at Reykjavík become the core of Iceland's first town.

1783 > Poisonous fallout from the gigantic Lakí eruptions in eastern Iceland sterilizes farms across the country, causing famines and killing a third of the population.

1787 > Denmark lifts the trade monopoly.

1835 > Jónas Hallgrímsson (and later Jón Sigurðsson) champions the idea of Icelandic nationalism and independence from Denmark.

1843 > The Danish king approves reconstitution of the Alþing at Reykjavík.

1871 > Denmark annexes Iceland.

1904 > Home Rule: Denmark grants political independence to Iceland.

1918 > Iceland becomes an independent Danish state.

1940-45 > During World War II, British and US forces occupy Iceland. After Denmark is captured by the Nazis, Iceland declares itself fully independent on June 17, 1944.

1949-51 > As the Cold War gains momentum, Iceland joins NATO and the US opens an airbase at Keflavík.

1958-85 > Iceland gradually expands its territorial waters to a two-hundred-mile (320km) radius around the country, sparking a series of "Cod Wars" with Britain over fishing rights.

1994 > Iceland becomes part of Europe, but stops short of joining the EU.

1998-2008 > Unregulated attempts to diversify the economy away from fishing by investing in banking creates a financial bubble which implodes in 2008, leaving twenty percent of Icelanders bankrupt.

2010 > The Eyjafjallajökull volcano erupts in a mighty ash cloud, causing aviation chaos in Europe – and bringing Iceland's raw landscape to the attention of international tourism.

2011-2015 > Tourist numbers grow twenty percent annually, reaching nearly a million visitors in 2015 – compared with a national population of just 329,000. Tourism becomes the biggest single source of revenue.

Language

Icelandic is a medieval language, retaining much of the complex grammar that has largely dropped out of use elsewhere in Europe. And while you might even recognize a few dialect nouns – tjörn for tarn (small pond), fjall for fell (mountain) – the pronunciation will leave you reeling (fjall is pronounced "fyatl", for example). Fortunately most Icelanders speak English, alongside other Nordic languages and a smattering of French and German; as they don't expect foreigners to know a word of Icelandic you'll delight everyone by attempting even the simplest phrase.

There are 32 letters in the Icelandic alphabet, including Þ (þ) and Ð (ð) – both, to all intents and purposes, pronounced "th". Bizarrely, there is no exact Icelandic equivalent for the word "interesting" – the closest being *gaman*, fun.

An idea of pronunciation is given in brackets.

BASIC WORDS AND PHRASES

I don't understand	ég skil ekki (yairg skil ekee)
Could you speak more slowly?	gætirðu talað hægar? (gye-tiroo talath hyegar)
Do you speak English?	talarðu ensku? (talarthoo enskoo)
Yes	já (yau)
No	nei (nay)
Hello	hæ (hi)
Good morning/ afternoon	góðan dag (go-than dargh)
Good night	góða nótt (go-tha not)
Goodbye	bless
Please	afsakið (afsakith)
Thank you	takk fyrir
What's your name?	hvað heitirðu? (kvath haytiroo?)
I'd like...	ég ætla að fá (yairg aytla ath fau)
Excuse me	fyrirgefðu (fyrir gef thoo)
How much does it cost?	hvað kostar þetta? (kvath kostar thetta?)
Where	hvar (kvar)
Toilet	snyrting
Men/women	karlmenn/kvenmenn
Open/closed	opið/lokað (opith/lokath)
Bill/check, please	reikninginn, takk

FOOD AND DRINK

arctic char	bleikja
beer	bjór
bread	brauð
burger	hamborgari
butter	smjör
cheese	ostur
cod	þorskur
coffee	kaffi
egg	egg
fermented shark	hákarl
fish	fiskur
herring	síld
hot dog	pylsur
Icelandic vodka	brennivín
Icelandic yoghurt	skyr
lamb	lamb
lobster	humar
milk	mjólk
pancakes, flatbread	laufabrauð, flatbrauð
pepper	pipar
pizza	pítsa
ptarmigan	rjúpa
reindeer	hreindýr
salmon	lax
salt	salt
skimmed milk	lettmjólk
smoked lamb	hangikjöt
soup	súpa
"steam bread"	hverabrauð
sugar	sykur
tea	te
trout	silungur
water	vatn
wind-dried cod	harðfiskur

PUBLISHING INFORMATION

This first edition published April 2016 by **Rough Guides Ltd**

80 Strand, London WC2R 0RL

11, Community Centre, Panchsheel Park, New Delhi 110017, India

Distributed by Penguin Random House

Penguin Books Ltd, 80 Strand, London WC2R 0RL

Penguin Group (USA) 345 Hudson Street, NY 10014, USA

Penguin Group (Australia) 250 Camberwell Road, Camberwell, Victoria 3124, Australia

Penguin Group (NZ) 67 Apollo Drive, Mairangi Bay, Auckland 1310, New Zealand

Penguin Group (South Africa) Block D, Rosebank Office Park, 181 Jan Smuts Avenue, Parktown North, Gauteng, South Africa 2193

Rough Guides is represented in Canada by

Tourmaline Editions Inc., 662 King Street West, Suite 304, Toronto, Ontario, M5V 1M7

Typeset in Minion and Din to an original design by Henry Iles and Dan May.

Printed and bound in China

© Rough Guides, 2016

Maps © Rough Guides. Map bases derived from OpenStreetMap (© OpenStreetMap contributors)

144pp includes index

A catalogue record for this book is available from the British Library

ISBN 978-0-24124-865-2

The publishers and authors have done their best to ensure the accuracy and currency of all the information in **Pocket Rough Guide Reykjavík**, however, they can accept no responsibility for any loss, injury, or inconvenience sustained by any traveller as a result of information or advice contained in the guide.

1 3 5 7 9 8 6 4 2

MIX
Paper from
responsible sources
FSC™ C018179
www.fsc.org

ROUGH GUIDES CREDITS

Editor: Neil McQuillian

Layout: Jessica Subramanian

Cartography: James Macdonald

Picture editor: Phoebe Lowndes

Photographer: Diana Jarvis

Proofreader: Jan McCann

Managing editor: Monica Woods

Production: Jimmy Lao

Cover photo research: Aude Vauconsant

Editorial assistant: Freya Godfrey

Senior pre-press designer: Dan May

Publisher: Keith Drew

Publishing director: Georgina Dee

ABOUT THE AUTHORS

David Leffman was born and raised in the UK, spent twenty years in Australia, then relocated back to Britain in 2009. Since 1992 he has authored and co-authored guides to Australia, China, Indonesia, Iceland and Hong Kong for Rough Guides, Dorling Kindersley and others, ghostwritten a Chinese cookbook and contributed articles for various publications on subjects ranging from crime to martial arts and history. If he had spare time he'd go scuba diving.

James Proctor is co-author of the Rough Guides to Iceland, Sweden and Finland, and has also written the only English-language guides to the Faroe Islands and Lapland. Having lived and worked in the Nordic countries in the mid-1990s as the BBC's Scandinavia correspondent, James willingly travels north at any opportunity – clearly a Viking in a past life. One of his more obscure talents is speaking several Nordic languages.

ACKNOWLEDGEMENTS

James Proctor would like to thank Kristbjörn and Ólafur in Reykjavik who helped tremendously with this new Pocket guide – not just with heaps of great ideas and suggestions but with providing a fun place to stay whilst in town. And thanks, too, for tracking down an Icelandic keyboard for me! Editor, Neil, also deserves special thanks for professionally pulling things together in the office.

HELP US UPDATE

We've gone to a lot of effort to ensure that the first edition of the **Pocket Rough Guide Reykjavík** is accurate and up-to-date. However, things change – places get "discovered", opening hours are notoriously fickle, restaurants and rooms raise prices or lower standards. If you feel we've got it wrong or left something out, we'd like to know, and if you can remember the address, the price, the hours, the phone number, so much the better.

Please send your comments with the subject line "**Pocket Rough Guide Reykjavík Update**" to mail@roughguides.com. We'll credit all contributions and send a copy of the next edition (or any other Rough Guide if you prefer) for the very best emails.

Find more travel information, connect with fellow travellers and book your trip on
Ⓦ roughguides.com

PHOTO CREDITS

Index

Maps are marked in **bold**.

Explore Iceland
with great value car hire

↻ **Compare** over 50 car rental companies in one click.

🔍 **Search** 2.5 Million+ locations worldwide

📅 **Book** early and save up to 40%*

Carrentals.co.uk
Let us do the hard work for you

*40% savings possible for bookings made over 4 weeks in advance